Firestarter

Firestarter

Igniting Change Through Leadership

C. ELLIOTT HAVERLACK

NAPLES, FL

Copyright © 2024 by C. Elliott Haverlack
All rights reserved

Published in the United States by O'Leary Publishing
www.olearypublishing.com

The views, information, or opinions expressed in this book are solely those of the authors involved, and do not necessarily represent those of O'Leary Publishing, LLC.

The author has made every effort possible to ensure the accuracy of the information presented in this book. However, the information herein is sold without warranty, either expressed or implied. Neither the author, publisher, nor any dealer or distributor of this book will be held liable for any damages caused either directly or indirectly by the instructions or information contained in this book. You are encouraged to seek professional advice before taking any action mentioned herein.

All rights reserved. No part of this book may be reproduced or transmitted in any form by any means: electronic, mechanical, photocopy, recording, or other, without the prior and express written permission of the author, except for brief cited quotes. For information on getting permission for reprints and excerpts, contact: O'Leary Publishing.

ISBN: (hardcover) 978-1-952491-66-5
ISBN: (ebook): 978-1-952491-63-4
Library of Congress Number: 2023916256

Developmental Editing by Heather Davis Desrocher
Line Editing by Boris Boland
Proofreading by Kat Langenheim
Cover and Interior Design by Jessica Angerstein
Printed in the United States of America

This work is dedicated to the mentors who guided me, and to the assistants who kept me grounded.

Julie, Cathy, and Cyndi – You gave unconditionally; and in turn, you enhanced my journey beyond my wildest expectations.

Ralph, Victor, and Dewey – Your inspiration and counsel helped me become the best version of the leader I was preordained to become.

Contents

Preface: A Firestarter ix

Introduction: A Born Leader? 1

BOOK 1
Leadership: The Responsibility to Ignite 9

    Chapter 1 So, You Want to Start Fires 15

    Chapter 2 The Kindling That Optimizes Combustion 37

    Chapter 3 Sourcing The Elements for Combustion 65

    Chapter 4 Smoke Signals 89

    Chapter 5 Spreading Like Wildfire – Your Wildfire 111

    Chapter 6 When The Fire is Doused 127

    Chapter 7 It's a Great Fire, But… 143

    Chapter 8 Tending the Fire 157

BOOK 2
Leading Teams: Letters that Burn 165

BOOK 3
Reflections: Leadership Ideas That Ignite 227

Epilogue: So Many Fires to Kindle 325

Acknowledgements 331

PREFACE

A Firestarter

Managers put out fires;
Leaders ignite them.

– Unknown

In all of history, the discovery of fire – more accurately, the discovery of the ability to start a fire – is cited as the pivotal point in the development of humanity. Imagine the excitement when the people of yesterday recognized that they could control something that had previously been an enigmatic conundrum. Up until that point in time, fire had been an uncontrollable detriment that destroyed people's food sources and disrupted their lives.

Controlled, it became a source of warmth, a protection against predators, and an illumination that brightened the evolutionary path into the future. Imagine the individual who exhibited the curiosity and courage to create that first spark that changed all of human history.

It is fascinating to reflect upon such a historical event. Someone, or maybe a few people, had the vision to explore the possibility. But there must have been significant fear among the broader community.

FIRESTARTER

It must have required a singular effort for the fire experimenters to influence the others into accepting the idea of harnessing the element.

These experimenters, these innovators, were the first leaders. Many of the principles that drove them are ensconced in the best leaders of today. Great leaders create an environment that enables ideas to flourish and become life-changing historical creations. Who might find the next cure? Who might invent the next transformative concept akin to the internet?

The development of leaders is an essential part of securing a brighter future for all of mankind. Leadership is singularly the most important factor in the success of an enterprise. Unfortunately, far too often, leadership and its vital significance is either misunderstood, overlooked, or underappreciated. A quick internet search reveals five billion results when the keyword "leadership" is entered. That is impressive, but it pales in comparison with another keyword "management." With over fifteen billion results, one might construe that management – not leadership – should win the day when discussing what is important in business.

It might be fair to ask: What is the difference? Does a manager not lead? Does a leader not manage? The answer to both questions is yes, but the subtlety of focusing on one compared to the other is a game-changer. Indeed, there are great leaders who struggle as managers. Similarly, there are exceptional managers that fail miserably at leading. Yet, in some instances, we find that rare individual who is exceptional in both areas – and success is the result. Maybe the best clarification is the following:

> Management is doing things right;
> leadership is doing the right things.
>
> – Peter F. Drucker

Preface

Some may use the words "management" and "leadership" interchangeably, but they are very different. Companies and individuals who focus on the principles of management tend to create cultures that are dull and uninspired. They restrain their teams with overbearing rules and regulations and create an overarching aura of **You Can't**. Yes, there is a place for policy and procedure. No company can operate without them, but when they circumvent elements such as focus, growth, and creativity, the business suffers and those vital attributes are stifled.

Comparatively, companies that favor leadership over management attract top talent that inspire their teams. They unlock innovation and embrace risk-taking, thus creating exciting and stimulating cultures. Embracing these concepts breathes life into the company. A culture of **What If** becomes embedded into the skin of the enterprise. **What If** is the quintessential example of a force multiplier; the energy feeds on itself, generating a powerful chain reaction.

Since every enterprise by definition has a leader, it is appropriate to conclude that there are throngs of bad leaders in top positions across the globe. The vast majority have not invested enough time nor energy in developing their leadership style. They have most likely not done the heavy lifting required to course-correct their weaknesses.

While many people may not be able to detail all the attributes and actions that make a great leader, nearly anyone can point to a leader and readily provide their perspective on that leader's effectiveness. We've all been there; we are drawn to leaders who inspire us, and we run from those who do not. Most of us can remember a time when we've been subjected to a leader who sucks all the air out of a room, making our existence intolerable.

Becoming a good leader, or what we will call a **Firestarter**, is not an accident. It takes great discipline. The development of leadership skills is a lifelong race – it is a marathon, not a sprint. While a leader cannot control every element of the journey, through discovery and dedication, he or she can make the path smoother, straighter, and more predictable.

Properly tended, the fire ignited by a good leader becomes inextinguishable. No water, no chemical, can quell the inferno – and the result will be an unprecedented achievement that leads to generational success. In the pages that follow, you will discover everything you need to kindle, fuel, and sustain the fire that already exists within you. You will learn how to fan the flames and extend the inferno throughout your enterprise.

A fair question might be: What will be my reward? Another might be: How do I know when I've arrived? The answer to both questions is the same. It is limitless fulfillment that extends beyond your work life. It will enrich your well-being and the well-being of those in your orbit. By constantly fostering an environment where spontaneous combustion is not only possible, but expected, powerful fires will ignite constantly, glowing with opportunity.

INTRODUCTION

A Born Leader?

*Do not follow where the path may lead.
Go instead where there is no path and leave a trail.*

– Ralph Waldo Emerson

We regularly hear, "He is a born leader" or "She is a born leader." Nothing could be further from the truth. Just as an elite athlete must undergo rigorous conditioning, becoming a great leader takes commitment, discipline, and years – if not decades – of training.

One's genetic makeup also affects how an individual might be predisposed to become a great leader or athlete. Examine the Manning family: a father and two sons, all likely to be enshrined in the Football Hall of Fame. The Mannings collectively provide a great example of the role that genetics plays. However, not one of them would have made it onto the field without countless hours of excruciating effort. They practiced when they were sick, they played when they were hurt, and they studied when they were exhausted.

Leaders are no different. If one wants to become a great leader, he or she must be prepared for a challenging road ahead. Unlike an athlete, whose professional career might span two decades, being a leader is a lifelong commitment. And in leadership, the game is not played on a finite grid nor in a specific setting. There is no arbitrary time limit and often the score is not known. Winning might take months – or even years.

Even more important, one can think that they are winning and not realize that their organization is fatally unhealthy until it is too late. Leadership plays out in the arena of life – it can be thankless, conflicting, and even cruel. It can also be exhilarating, rewarding, and educational. For a leader, the journey is symbiotic with life itself. Leadership is a fantastic expedition into the unknown, with countless stops along the way to enhance the trek.

What qualifies me to write a book on leadership? My career has spanned over 40 years, and throughout my working life, I have focused on education. I've been leading teams since my first day on the job, and I have been learning at every step along the way. At 64 years old, I find that I continue to hone my leadership style.

Am I a great leader? I suspect that the answer is subjective. The best way to know the answer to that question is to look at the results; so, by that standard, I have been effective.

Since I have rigorously invested in developing my leadership skills, I know that I am a better leader today than I was in the past. I was not born a leader; I had no driving force to become a leader. But early on, I was placed in a position where I was expected to lead – and I found it exhilarating. After that experience, I was drawn to roles where leadership was a key element.

The vast majority of my career centered around companion-animal nutrition, more commonly known as dog and cat food, and

Introduction

treats. Even though I was not born with a desire to nourish our canine and feline companions, it has become so hard-coded into my psyche now that it is fair to refer to me as an advocate turned evangelist. I love everything about it.

There is a fun saying we have in the industry: "Unless you are the lead dog, the scenery never changes." I suppose there is some truth to that; but if you want to become a great leader, you had better be prepared to spend a significant amount of time at the rear of the pack. Dogs are descended from wolves, and in a wolf pack, the leader instinctively knows what the role requires. It calls for nurturing, education, and gaining the support of the pack. The wolf pack leader recognizes that much of what they want to achieve will be fulfilled from the rear.

In the human world, leading from the rear means connecting with every team member and even picking up a broom when required. As the first one in the office on a snowy day, the true leader will shovel the sidewalk and spread the salt. And he or she will brew a pot of coffee for the team members who arrive chilled from exposure to the elements.

Another fun canine adage is, "You can't teach an old dog new tricks." Once again, that's not quite accurate. If a dog wants to lead, he or she had better come to work prepared to learn something new every day. Those **new tricks** learned along the career journey are tools that the leader can employ to enhance the experience for the team. And as the leader becomes an expert in using them, team members are more fulfilled in their roles.

Even the finest universities are ill-equipped to prepare their graduates for the dynamics of leadership. Textbooks cannot predict what a fresh-out-of-college, naive, budding leader might encounter. Company cultures are as varied as the stars in the night sky, and they range from enabling to toxic. Moreover, a corporate culture that one recruit finds ideal might be stifling to another.

One of the challenges for any emerging leader is to determine if the corporate culture at their place of employment is a fit for their value system. It can be a real struggle if there is not a match, and it might take years for the leader to muster the courage to seek a more aligned cultural environment.

The first 20 years of my career, I worked at companies where results were the only thing that really mattered. In those corporate cultures, the path one followed to deliver the results was not nearly as important as the achievement – the outcome.

Most of my co-workers considered those companies good places to work. Nevertheless, we worked under constant and unpleasant pressure. For example, at one company, colleagues were forced into competitive situations; if one employee won, that meant someone else had to lose. At one point, we even proudly described ourselves as Vikings. We loved the self-imposed moniker, and even joked that we "knew where the women and children were."

Yet, as I developed my leadership style, I worked tirelessly to shield my team from the dysfunction that was created by that culture. Other leaders chose to embrace the culture, and I could see that their teams suffered under authoritarian rule. Over time, I was able to attract the best and the brightest to my team and we easily delivered the results that were so emphatically demanded.

We celebrated our success; we basked in the fact that we were winners and others were not so lucky. Tragically, we missed the vital point – we never considered that there was plenty of opportunity for

Introduction

all of us to win. It just did not cross our minds. I often reflect on just how many opportunities were lost or under-realized then, due to our misguided corporate culture.

There were several other leaders who chose a similar path to the one that I took, and their results were equally impressive. They enjoyed great connectivity with their teams. Like me, they felt quite out of place in the "dog-eat-dog" culture.

Interestingly, the vast majority of leaders I worked with who chose a more culturally convenient path were often very good souls. That point was confirmed to me years later, when I met several of them at trade shows. By that time, they were all leading teams at different companies.

I barely recognized them; they had all gone through amazing metamorphoses. So, it had been the culture, not their lack of character, that led them to lead in a less-than-optimal fashion. Earlier, they had succumbed to the pressure of conforming; but now, those same men and women were free from their chains of mediocrity. As part of that release, their facial expressions, demeanors, and personas were completely transformed. They seemed to be completely different entities. They had gone from caterpillar to butterfly.

During the second half of my career, I was introduced to a completely different approach. In that workplace, culture was a living, breathing imperative that was constantly being developed and enhanced. It was a true shock, and I even commenced referring to the place as "la-la land." Over time, I became infatuated with the freedom and inspiration that the culture embraced. Results were measured, but our values were not compromised.

I remember a time when one of the leaders of the previous generation stopped into my office. Popping his feet on my conference table, he counseled me. "It's just dog food," he said. "It's going to be in the lawn in a few days." *Maybe – just maybe,* I thought – *being a Viking had a downside.*

I came to loathe the "Viking" concept and considered relegating it to the trash heap of my past; but I opted to celebrate that part of my growth as a leader. In doing so, I ensured that I would never allow myself to slip into such a negative way of thinking again.

The epiphany I experienced fueled an on-the-job performance that most would consider improbable, maybe even impossible. I had migrated from a system where there had to be **winners and losers** to one where there would be **winners and learners.** It truly was leadership reborn. The system I adopted has so driven my actions that I have become an ambassador for this style of leadership. Because I believe in it so much, I feel compelled to share my knowledge, wisdom and experience through this book.

Firestarter is a detailed primer on leadership principles. There are countless paths one might take to become a leader and a wide variety of leadership styles to consider. But there are key characteristics that define a great leader, and vital elements that bolster success. We will walk together through the trials – and down the trails – of leadership. In doing so, we will venture into a new world of possibilities where teams win. More importantly, in that new world, team members love every minute of the journey – even the challenging ones.

One of the best ways I know to lead effectively is to provide frequent communication. I often used written letters to connect with and encourage the teams I led. So, *Firestarter* includes reprints of some of the letters written by me to my teams over the past 20 years. It is my hope that the letters will inspire and reassure you, the leader.

Introduction

It is also my intention that you use the letters as templates to support communication with your teams. There is a letter for almost any situation that you may encounter. Having a great year? There is a letter that recognizes and thanks your people. Facing a challenge? There is a letter that comforts and reassures team members. Want to advance the company values? There is a letter that advocates for company values and challenges the team. One of the great things about letters is since they are in print, they stand as an eternal record.

The book ends with selected educational articles that were originally shared on various social media platforms. These articles are snippets of vital concepts that will change your perspective and unlock a world of possibilities. They can have a lasting impact on your style. Each short article includes seeds of contentment that will develop into team well-being. We are educators first and always, and the articles contain essential educational nuggets that will stimulate the creative juices – without an undue time investment.

My intention is to ignite a fire within you that is not extinguishable – and that fire will also transform you into an igniter. A leader from yesteryear inciting a passion in those who will take teams into the future – that is the goal. The matches are contained in the pages that follow. Let's ignite together.

BOOK 1

Leadership: The Responsibility to Ignite

The greatest leader is not necessarily
the one who does the greatest things.

He is the one that gets the people
to do the greatest things.

~ Ronald Reagan

From *You Can't* to *What If*

However we become a leader, whether the process is purposeful or serendipitous, we find ourselves with an awesome responsibility. Equipped with a set of rules or expectations, we step out into a new world. But we as new leaders are likely ill-equipped for the travails that lie ahead.

In business and in life, there are objectives – and sometimes there is little ambiguity. For example, if it is your job to lead a team to paint a house, the objective is rather clear. How that objective is achieved is the responsibility of the leader. Once the project is completed, a judgment on its success or failure is fairly straightforward. Is the house painted? Is the job of acceptable quality? Was the job completed in the time expected? Was the work done within acceptable cost parameters?

In this basic example, we see principles that might be the game-changer for long-term success. Assuming that the answer to the questions in the previous paragraph is yes, we can ask ourselves some more subtle questions. How did the team feel about you as their leader? Will they be inclined to work for you in the future? More importantly, given other options, would they be inclined to continue working for you? Other than the obvious economic incentives, what else did they receive from you that will help their quality of life? Did you educate? Did you motivate? Were you empathetic?

While those are all great questions, many might not even consider them when examining such a basic task. When we start asking such questions at the basic level, they become ingrained into our psyche. After that occurs, it is far easier to handle the most complex of leadership roles.

Another example of a leadership situation might be one that involves a middle school basketball coach – which is a volunteer leadership position. In that case, we might think that the objective is clear – to teach the players the game of basketball. Yet another objective might be to win a championship.

I can speak from experience here. I took on that exact role – and considering that I knew nothing about basketball, it was a daunting task. But in my case, the objective was clear: educate and equip young souls to compete in life. Using basketball as the backdrop, I set out to teach teamwork, integrity, discipline, and responsibility. It was equally important to me to ensure that each of the players had fun and would become the best possible version of themselves – on and off the court. If we ended up winning the championship, so be it. I saw that scenario as only a peripheral outcome.

In my opinion, youth sports and professional sports are very different. In professional sports, adults are paid significant sums of money and their objective should be to win the championship each year. Nevertheless, professional players are profoundly influenced by the training they received from coaches in their youth. As pros, they still may exhibit values learned from their coaches while they were in their teens. Are they team players? Do they exhibit integrity? Are they disciplined? Do they take responsibility?

Book 1 Leadership: The Responsibility to Ignite

If the answer to the previous four questions is "no," then the leaders of their youth failed them. If that has happened, even the most talented professional athletes will most likely fail to achieve a championship. Or when they do win a championship, it is in spite of their shortcomings.

Leadership is all about inspiring teams to be better than they would be without the leader's guidance. As they respond to a leader's vision, team members experience the exhilaration of achieving the seemingly impossible. **What If,** through your singular leadership style, thousands – or millions – of lives are positively impacted? Yes, leaders can change lives, and their influence can extend well beyond the obvious.

Many of the fondest moments in my career occurred when I was able to watch my team members soar higher than they ever believed they could. There is no greater reward than having that team member confirm that your leadership style unlocked something special in their psyche. It's so fulfilling to know that the empowerment you gave them was the driving force that made everything possible.

In the pages that follow, we will discover the ingredients required to kindle the leadership fire. We will define the spark that ignites the spirit, examine the fuel essential to keep it burning, and analyze what it takes to educate a new generation of firestarters. Our young firestarters will blaze their own trails and illuminate their own journeys. We will migrate from the mundane world of **You Can't,** and unlock a wondrous universe full of **What If.**

CHAPTER 1

So, You Want to Start Fires

There is no passion to be found playing small;
in settling for a life that is less than the one
you are capable of living.

– Nelson Mandela

At many points in our life journey, we are faced with decisions. Some decisions are rather mundane; others can turn out to be transformative. A decision to assume the role of a leader is one that should be carefully considered.

Once you are a leader, then what? Unless you have carefully considered what it takes to be a good leader, there are a few possible outcomes. You could simply fail. You could become an uninspiring leader who muddles through every situation to deliver ordinary results. Or, you could turn out to be a very quick learner with a leadership style that strongly motivates your people.

You must decide what type of leader you want to be. Often, aspiring leaders use personal experiences to dial in the attributes that they find most desirable. Both good experiences and bad ones are relevant to building a leadership style.

Theoretically, the new generation of leaders will strive to avoid observed leadership behavior that they found objectionable. The hope is that they will instead foster leadership behavior that they believe is positive. But far too often, I have seen an aspiring leader adopt the same poor behaviors exhibited by leaders they disliked. The ideal approach is to find a leadership style that delivers the results you seek, without compromising your core values.

But what are core values?

The Importance of Values

Core values are a collection of guiding principles – principles that guide the way you live your life. Once assembled, they become the essential elements that make up your moral compass. The moral compass is that wayfinder – that essential tool – in helping you traverse your life journey.

Determining and reflecting upon what values are core to your existence is an essential exercise. The core values are driving forces that fuel your personal drive and lead to well-being. For example, one of my core values is education. If I am not teaching or being taught, I feel like there is something missing in my life. Along with education, I value curiosity. For me, those two values go hand in hand. My curiosity leads me to more opportunities to become educated; and in turn, my own education equips me to educate others.

Every company should purposefully commit to creating a set of core values. And, it is optimal that a leader in a company's organization and the company itself are aligned on value systems.

The topic of speed can provide a great example of how core values can be misaligned. If the company values speed, and that value is embedded into the skin of the enterprise, a company leader who finds speed unimportant or unnecessary will likely be viewed as dull or ordinary.

Conversely, if a leader truly values speed in his or her core and the company does not or cannot embrace that value, the leader might be viewed as irresponsible or reckless. That perception could easily transcend into fear, which could run rampant through the organization.

Motivation Matters

The next element for a good leader to consider is motivation. What is your reason for seeking a position in leadership? There are motives behind almost everything we do; there could be any number of motives that compel our actions. Very possibly, we could experience multiple motivations simultaneously. If I stop into a convenience store to grab a bottle of water, was thirst my motivation? Was I compelled by a desire to remain hydrated? Quite possibly, I simply needed the water to take some required medications.

In many cases, we are not honest about our motives. That disconnect can happen when our desires conflict with our moral compass or when we are acting out of fear. Desire and fear exert strong influences that can override our moral compass.

Desire can be an almost irresistible compulsion. While we might know that an action is physically, mentally, or spiritually unhealthy, we often choose it anyway. Acting on addiction is the perfect example of an unhealthy desire overriding a moral compass. We know that something addictive is harmful; yet, we are unable to resist.

And, if we look beyond the traditionally recognized addictions, we can see that we must also be vigilant that we do not become addicted to power, fame, or wealth. Those addictions can be even more detrimental than the more obvious ones, because it is often difficult to see their downside at first.

Overcoming fear is a paradox. We might think that our fear is completely within our control, yet we are unable to shake its grasp. Fear might be one of the greatest challenges a person can overcome.

It is a lifelong struggle to keep desire in check and to overcome fear, but through continual self-reflection, we can render both emotions inconsequential.

Once you have an awareness of your desires and your fears, you can then look more clearly at what motivates you to become a leader. There is no right answer, but there are plenty of wrong or unhealthy motivations that might compel you to accept a position of leadership.

I coach quite a few younger people, and one of the first questions I ask them is: "What do you want to achieve in your lifetime?" Almost universally, the answer is wealth, and most add either fame or power. Many have the vision to describe, in detail, what being rich means. One young man described "rich" as including a private jet and a vacation home in Telluride. At age 20, he had it all figured out – or so he thought.

When I probe them as to exactly why they want to seek wealth, fame or power, the answers always seem to become less clear. In many cases, they are unable to describe their rationale. They just know they want to be rich. They see wealth as symbiotic with a great quality of life.

To help them clarify their vision, I ask, "What if your goal was to become the best version of you? What if achieving this status led to

Book 1 Leadership: The Responsibility to Ignite

wealth and fame? Would that be OK?" Normally, the response will be smiles, head nods, and yeses.

I then continue: "What if you never achieved wealth or fame, but still found fulfillment? What if you looked back and saw that your life was abundant in experiences? What if you made a positive difference in the lives of others? What if you left the world in a better place than you found it?" When I ask those questions, I usually get confused looks. Many are not so sure what the optimal path for them would be.

As we mature, we become more comfortable with thinking about such important questions. We realize that leadership is not about wealth, power, or fame. Indeed, all three can be outcomes of acting as an effective leader. But if you are solely motivated by wealth, power, or fame, it is likely that you will either not achieve those ends or follow an unhealthy path that leads to discontent. When your goal is to become the best version of the person you were meant to be, fulfillment and abundance are your natural rewards. I believe that the type of motivation that a leader has is the most important element that predicts whether he or she will become great.

I also like to ask people, "What if, after achieving success, you were left feeling unfulfilled?" or "What if you found fortune, fame and power, but you had to trample on the lives of others to achieve it? Would that be a satisfactory outcome?" I think that most of us could create a list of leaders down through history who embodied such egomania. They are the pariahs of history.

Hitler is the poster child of what can happen when there is a blind desire to achieve ultimate power at any price. Initially, he was a charismatic and effective leader who electrified a beleaguered populace that was yearning for hope. World War I had left Germany battered and beaten. The nation's economy had descended into the abyss, and hopelessness was omnipresent. Desperate, the citizens followed Hitler's appealing message. History likes to gloss over the fact that many world leaders of that day sympathized with the plight of the Germans and – at first – supported Hitler's philosophy. But as history has taught us, the very skills that made Hitler effective emboldened him, and the result was unprecedented horror.

What were Hitler's initial motivations? And did his motivations evolve as his tainted mind fueled his megalomania? What motivated the German people? Most likely, it was fear. With the country in such dire circumstances, most Germans must have questioned the future of their existence. Hitler seemed to offer hope and answers.

Why is Hitler relevant to our discussion of leadership? The answer is simple. He illustrates how the temptations of leadership, coupled with a flawed value system, can create a disaster. Indeed, leaders regularly become punch-drunk on power and status. In the worst cases, they become addicted to the position and the supremacy, and to all the comforts that are part of the total package. Their judgment is clouded by a world of private jets, limousines, and teams of subordinates that exist solely to serve their every need. In the worst cases, the mission becomes more about the leader than the organization they serve.

We see such scenarios play out publicly with television evangelists. Jim and Tammy Faye Bakker might be the best example of a pair of evangelists who lost their way.

I have no quarrel with evangelism. Most evangelists are great people who are genuine in their belief systems. In fact, I consider myself an evangelist of sorts. Moreover, private jets, limousines, and support staff can be essential elements that enable a leader to accomplish great results. Nevertheless, the leader must ensure that their perspective does not become sullied.

Book 1 Leadership: The Responsibility to Ignite

What You See Is Not What You Get

One reason that it is important to be clear about your motivation for choosing a leadership role is that leadership is much harder than it looks. There are many unseen aspects to it. When it becomes challenging, a clear and powerful motivation is what will sustain you. Many see an office job as a world of opulence, status, and wealth, but they fail to comprehend that – just like an iceberg floating in the North Atlantic – what they perceive is only a small piece of the whole. On the surface, leadership roles appear rather enticing, but there are elements that can be excruciating. There are responsibilities that will keep a leader up at night – and crises that can shake you to the core.

Issues involving product integrity and employee layoffs are examples of meaningful situations that will require a leader to agonize and reflect. In such internal or unseen struggles, a leader must appear unflappable. Yet, the leader's outward persona can be misconstrued by others as uncaring or disconnected.

There is also always competition in any industry, and in many ways there are few rules for dealing with rivals. It can almost become a blood sport. We see gamesmanship and ruthlessness play out in politics on an ongoing basis. Truth be damned, gaining power is the only goal, and how that power is achieved is of no consequence. Depending on where you are in your career journey, you have likely seen such actions in real time.

The starkest example of competition in my career came when I was a young, naive 20-something. A new Human Resources assistant manager was hired to support the company's growing needs in that area. He was charming and initially appeared to be deeply committed to enhancing the culture.

Stupidly, I waded into his trap. Under the guise of confidentiality, he lured me into conversations about his boss and spoon-fed me fictitious notions. I soon found out that he had been doing the same thing with others. He sprung his trap and released a damning report with all the gory details.

What was his motivation? He wanted to discredit his supervisor and take his place as head of Human Resources. The plan failed and he was reassigned to another facility, but not before causing irreparable damage to many, including his supervisor – who was also reassigned. For me, it became a great teachable moment, and while I suffered greatly as a result of the ordeal, I was able to use the lesson to enhance my overall acumen.

A Healthy Foundation

A successful leader must be committed to health – personal health, team health, and cultural health. Only through an intense focus on health can the individual, the team, or the culture realize the pinnacle of excellence.

In personal health we look at physical health, mental health, and spiritual health. Physical health is rather straightforward. It is a combination of inputs and outputs. The inputs include food, drink, and other things we allow into our bodies. Are we committed to a rather healthy diet? Do we smoke? Do we drink alcohol? Do we have a drug dependency?

Smoking has been shown to be unhealthy and seems irresponsible to me. The same is true for the excessive intake of alcohol. Drinking alcoholic beverages in moderation is a perfectly acceptable part of an overall healthy lifestyle. But excessive alcohol consumption certainly will not contribute to overall health or well-being.

The other aspect of physical health is an output – exercise. As with the inputs, an exercise regime is subjective. However, a total lack of attention to exercise will lead to poor overall health. Many people will

Book 1 Leadership: The Responsibility to Ignite

say that they have no time to commit to a robust exercise program. I would counter that committing to exercise actually creates time, and allows you to control your schedule. When we adopt a healthier lifestyle, we find that we spend less time visiting doctors, take fewer sick days, and have fewer illnesses that hinder performance.

Mental health is an important and often misunderstood element of a healthy lifestyle. Is your psyche healthy? Do you experience anxiety? Are you comfortable in your own skin? These are some of the questions that should be asked and answered. When an organization does not foster mental health, negative emotion can creep into the organization. Such emotion can generate reactionary responses, which can crush organizational cooperation.

While emotion is debilitating, passion is empowering. When mental health is championed, passion is unlocked, which leads to a purposeful drive to achieve goals. Focusing on mental health fosters passion and helps keep emotion in check. We rarely hear the term "a passionate outburst," but "an emotional outburst" is well understood, and almost always is accompanied by negative and unintended consequences.

Equally important is spiritual health. Do you have a good grasp on where you fit into the broader society? What is your driving force? More importantly, do you know why you are so driven?

I feel that as a Christian, spiritual health is easily understood. I believe I have a good handle on where I fit in and why I am driven in the direction I am. That said, another leader can have a very healthy spiritual relationship and follow a different faith – or no definite faith at all. Belief in the existence of a divine creator is truly one of the great mysteries, but if such a belief is not reconciled within one's spirit, it can lead to challenges.

It is essential that a leader commits to physical, mental, and spiritual health. Then, when tragedies occur, a healthy leader can traverse misfortunes with ease. Balanced leaders can efficiently shepherd the team through them, leaving the team better for having had the experience.

Essential Leader Magnification Tools

Do you remember the first time you looked in a microscope and brought an unseen world into focus? I remember delighting in the protozoans dancing on my slide. There were dozens of them – it was an entire world thriving in an environment no larger than a pinhead. How about your first experience using a telescope, or your first visit to a planetarium? Wasn't it fascinating?

In leadership, "telescopes" and "microscopes" are very different metaphors, but also share much in common. Both tools allow us to see things that are otherwise invisible. The telescope is often employed by great leaders. Most agree that the telescope is a great tool to envision those things that are on the horizon.

The microscope does not have as broad an appeal in the context of leadership. We often hear horror stories about micromanagers who debilitate team members. Micromanagement is a valid concern in a workplace, and the temptation to micromanage should be carefully considered.

However, the metaphorical microscope can be a valuable leadership tool. It enhances root-cause analysis and may answer "the question behind the question." Indeed, it is not often good enough to learn why something occurred. It's the "why behind the why" that will lead us to the true root of an issue. Magnification can regularly bring the unobservable into focus; then, solutions can be created.

Only after close examination can we ensure that nagging issues are thoroughly vetted.

For example: we learn that the company's plant lost 12 hours of production. Why? Well, a gearbox broke. What made the gearbox break? We do not know. We might theorize that any of a number of root causes caused the issue. But if we do not pull out our microscope and determine the responsible issue, it is likely to recur.

Skilled leaders must become adept in the use of both the microscope and the telescope. Knowing when each should be employed – along with knowing the level of intensity to be used – is a key to enhancing success. While it sounds easy on the surface, a misappropriated use of either tool can create chaos and lead to dysfunction. Becoming a master navigator and inspector is important. Developing those skills as a leader requires a discerning eye and a steady hand.

How I Caught Fire

One of the best ways to become an effective leader is to learn what has worked for others on their leadership paths and apply those principles. It is my intent to offer information in this book that will make you better equipped to follow a path to leadership – one that can be purposeful and empowering. So, let me share the story of my journey. Rather than being an ideal model to emulate, it is more of an unlikely tale with plenty of avoidable twists.

My journey into leadership was quite serendipitous. I was married, graduated from college, and I wanted to be an environmental scientist. I truly believed that I was destined to solve some of the biggest environmental challenges of our time. Moreover, I intended to achieve my success from the field as opposed to working in a laboratory. I was thinking on a rather large scale, but seeing myself in a leadership role was not part of the vision.

I wanted to save the world, but I quickly learned that the world really did not want to be saved – at least not by me. The job market was challenging, and the type of position I sought was unavailable – or at a minimum, not addressable. I found myself in the position of management trainee on the night shift in the largest bakery in Pittsburgh. If the truth be told, at that time I would have accepted almost any position available.

So, the scientist became a leader. I absolutely hated the working conditions at the bakery, but I loved the challenge. It was a true paradox. The treatment of the people in the workplace was intolerable; so, in return, the team members repaid management with substandard performance.

It was about a year before I found a chance to truly make some changes. When I did, success ensued. Within another year, the team – my team – went from being the brunt of jokes to the most sought-after unit in the company. We posted wins across the board – so much so, that I was rewarded with fantastic trips.

The incentive program was designed to reward, but was so tightly structured that it was nearly impossible to receive repeat benefits. My teams, however, were so good that they helped me win a second trip and then a third. We won an unprecedented six awards. We won so often that I even gave one of the trips to a team member, who I felt exemplified the qualities of a leader. The success fed on itself, and I found that I absolutely loved winning (as part of a team). More importantly, I loved watching the delight of the team members as they won and were rewarded for their efforts.

Book 1 Leadership: The Responsibility to Ignite

I learned some very valuable lessons in my early years as a leader. I suppose that the most important one was that many people have never tasted success, and in turn, only believed that it was reserved for others. Most of my team had grown up in the less desirable sections of the city. They had been subjected to intolerable circumstances, and, I thought, a cruel brainwashing. Almost every member of my team knew someone who was in prison. In many cases, the imprisoned person was someone in their immediate family.

I learned that with even a tiny taste of victory, amazing things can occur. The impossible became possible. The possible became probable. The probable became reality. We truly expected to win – and we did. In fact, I do not recall a failure from that team for over three years. It was absolutely astounding, and I began to embrace the art of the possible.

During my time there, I reported to five different bosses: one was terrible, one was poor, two were very good, and one was excellent. The last one became a mentor, and I continue to embrace many of the leadership skills he taught me to this day. Nearly 40 years later, the experiences from that first position – both good and bad – still influence my moral compass. On one hand, I have been blessed by my hard-wired commitment to education; on the other hand, I remain repulsed by the intolerable treatment I witnessed and personally experienced.

A transfer to New Jersey came; it left me reeling and uninspired. My new superior was an intelligent man; and I believe that he was a man of great integrity, but he did not possess the leadership attributes I saw as essential. Partly because of that, I sought different employment. I found what appeared to be a great position with a notable company, yet my career path was still unclear.

The new position was located in Biloxi, Mississippi, where the cost of living was nearly half of what it had been in New Jersey. And, the reduced expense was coupled with a 40 percent pay increase. I came up with a new plan that involved my interest in environmental science: I would work and save money so I could return to school. My goal was to be a chemistry teacher at the collegiate level; I even created a detailed five-year plan, like any good leader would.

But within a few months in my new role, I became addicted to the excitement and challenges of leadership. It was my first role leading an entire site. We were winning so much that the aura of success spread throughout the enterprise. Our work led to two promotions and two moves for me in a period of just eight months.

It was then I realized that I wanted to run a company. I literally lusted for the exhilaration that came with leadership roles. Winning was important, but the way that we would win was paramount. Admittedly, I experienced some extraordinarily difficult periods as I grew as a leader. However, the difficulties were soon relegated to the recesses of my mind as my team members and I leapt the hurdles in our path.

Before I knew it, I was on the management board of two divisions of a Fortune 500 company and had around 1,000 people working for me. If contract workers were included, the number was closer to 2,000.

Eight moves in 11 years wore on my family. The final move was to my hometown of Pittsburgh. Initially, I was delighted, but I found my new boss to be a man of suspect character. I believed him to embody the antithesis of almost every admirable leadership principle, so I simply walked away.

I was 41 – and the prospect of starting over was exhilarating.

Book 1 Leadership: The Responsibility to Ignite

I secured a position in a sleepy little company where I had to change my perspective, and it was an adjustment. I went from approving million-dollar expenditures to overseeing transactions in the thousands. More significantly, I became exposed to a culture that was very foreign to me – a culture of family, where lifting others up was encouraged (versus my previous experience, where others were threatened or cut down). I found that I loved my new world, and I immediately embraced it.

Gone was the Viking. In his place emerged a builder and a unifier. Still, no corporate culture is perfect, and in this new one I found very little accountability and very little attention to results. Timelines were missed, results were substandard, and the true concept of winning was not even a consideration.

After a month on the job, I approached the owner and advised him that we would triple the company's business within three years. He literally laughed at me and jokingly threw me out of his office. But a year and a half later, we **had** tripled the business – and by Year 5, we had doubled the business again. Within a decade, we saw revenues swell 15-fold and profits soared. We had gone from being a punchline of the industry into the sixth-largest entity in our field.

What was the secret sauce? It was vision and capability, fueled by confidence and courage. Previously, the company had not seen itself as particularly capable and was content to plod along as it had for the previous 68 years. The company helped support the lives of 200 families, and the owners enjoyed a very affluent lifestyle. By all accounts, things were good. As Jim Collins, the noteworthy author of several groundbreaking business books counsels, "Good is the enemy of Great." So, it was... but we lit a fire in the company that was inextinguishable. It was exhilarating. We expected to win, and we did.

Along the way, we made two acquisitions. We saw both as enhancements to our core mission. They were distressed organizations, and we were able to secure a controlling interest in both for nominal investments.

One was on the cusp of bankruptcy. Its leadership was weak and divisive, and within a few short months we were facing some very difficult decisions. The chief financial officer had been discharged in conjunction with our acquisition, and then we felt we had no option but to part ways with the president too. I found myself immersed in the dysfunction – and became the new president.

Because I was only on site one week per month at the organization, it was not the ideal situation for me to make improvements. Even so, slowly, we were able to turn the ship into much smoother sailing. The company continued to underperform, but at least we were financially stable. *Maybe this is good enough,* I thought. Then I heard the words of Jim Collins echoing in my mind, and I realized that the people and the investors deserved better.

We engaged a consultant. After her initial fact-finding, she advised me that the team was suffering from a lack of trust – maybe the worst case of it that she'd ever encountered. So, we developed a plan to build trust and to purposefully plot our plan to win. All the key decision-makers gathered for a planning session. Over a three-day period, we developed a strategic plan that included defining our mission, vision and values. We employed a multifaceted communication and marketing campaign to ensure all stakeholders, both internal and external, became well acquainted with our newly created vision and the details of how we intended to make it a reality.

We started to experience a groundswell of positivity. The company was extraordinarily busy, yet there still seemed to be something a bit off. The team had been working countless hours, and I suspected that

Book 1 Leadership: The Responsibility to Ignite

it might be causing some angst on the home front with the workers' families. In an attempt to build more trust, I announced that I had scheduled a three-day, offsite meeting – with spouses included. I suspected that some of the employees were having some trepidation as we embarked on our trip – the destination was New Orleans.

To confirm that the trip's official purpose was business, we had a two-hour meeting the first morning. But the rest of the three-day getaway was a giant party with lavish dinners, team-building events, and – most importantly – music. As I look back on it, those three days did more for trust and team dynamics than any other event in my career. One important thing in particular happened: we achieved buy-in from the spouses, since they had been invited. The team-building trip became an annual event, and we found ourselves going to some of the most amazing venues in the United States.

Trust continued to build, and we realized that we were achieving our vision in much less time than expected. We found ourselves back in the planning mode. Our vision had become our mission, and our new vision was even more aspirational than the previous one. Our next strategic planning cycle was the most exceptional one I had ever experienced. It was also the easiest and least expensive. It became my template for excellence in planning.

While my day job was becoming more complex, the subsidiary's business grew. We decided that we needed new, full-time leadership there. The owners of my company directed me to commence a quiet search; I agreed to the search, but refused to make it silent. I would not throw two years of team-building and trust out the window.

The team members assembled in the conference room. I advised them that I had important news, and that I would not be taking questions in the group format. Furthermore, I had scheduled hour-long, one-on-one conferences with each stakeholder.

"I have been asked to find a new leader for the company," I told them; and then I added, "…and it's none of you." I explained that I had been asked to perform the leadership search in secrecy, but that I had not agreed to keep it under wraps. I closed the meeting with, "I know you will all make me relish the decision to advise you personally, and in advance."

There were six team members at the meeting, and three had the courage to ask me to consider them for the position. I gave them strict guidelines on what they would need to do to be considered. Most importantly, I advised them to start acting like leaders immediately. Within two months, one person from the team, a woman, emerged as my lead candidate. My superiors were skeptical; but I insisted, and they acquiesced.

The decision to place this woman in the leadership role is the best people decision of my career. I had never seen her as a leader, but she grabbed the mantle of leadership and excelled. She was a true visionary. Her vision for the company catapulted what we had already accomplished to an unprecedented level. The right person in the right role is a game changer, and she was a living, breathing example.

Meanwhile, at the parent business, after a decade of triumph, we were faced with the reality of a significant failure. Our entire year was upended in an instant. In many ways, the situation was caused by our success – we allowed overconfidence to inflate our egos. We simply forgot to adequately safeguard the company, and it cost us.

It was yet another educational moment that I saw as an opportunity for growth and enlightenment. It took intense discipline and commitment by the team, but the ship was righted. Yet, at 53, and after 12 years at the job, I was mentally exhausted. As the president, I took personal responsibility for the failure.

Book 1 Leadership: The Responsibility to Ignite

While the company had a very bright future ahead, I again decided to walk away and start over. Despite being asked to stay on by the owners, I realized that it was time for new leadership. What we had accomplished had been noteworthy, but for the good of the company, I stepped down.

During that time, a different kind of fire was ignited within my psyche. I wanted to help others, so I created a consulting and life coaching company. I began speaking to audiences large and small about living a better life. And finally, I began writing books. I am not certain what the future holds, but I expect that it will be exciting – and that it will lead to further fulfillment.

When I reflect upon the entirety of my journey, it truly is a paradox. The shy young man who wanted nothing to do with leading people stepped into leadership out of desperation. But I found that leading people is my true life purpose, and I have thrived off the fires that have been ignited along the way. I found that in many cases, those fires – lighted and fostered by my teams – were inextinguishable. When I have returned to visit the arenas where I led during my career, I delight in experiencing the energy of the infernos ignited during my tenure. I am proud that those fires have been fueled and tended, decades after my departure.

Looking back, the memories that I cherish most involve the people I worked with, and their strong personalities. These are people living lives of abundance beyond their wildest expectations. What could be better?

An employee asked me once how she could ever thank me for what I had done for her career. I simply replied, "My thanks will come when it's your turn, and you do the same thing."

Now as I face my fourth retirement, I find myself drawn to people and helping them rise to leap the hurdles of life – helping them to excel. I doubt that I will ever truly retire. You can take the person out of the fire of leadership, but you cannot take the fire to lead out of the person.

Lighthearted Lesson: When to Exit Someone

At the end of each chapter, I will share experiences that teach a lighthearted lesson. I hope these stories will entertain you, as one of my guiding leadership principles is to simply… "Have Fun." Sometimes the realization that an employee is not a good fit can make for a humorous story. Here are two such stories.

One day, someone threw a garbage can at our shipping office window, shattering it. The perpetrator had entered the break area, smashed the glass in the vending machine, and stolen all the snacks inside.

The scene was rather grisly, as the robber had evidently cut himself or herself in the process of the theft. There was a significant amount of blood left behind. We also found a wallet lying near the window with identification inside. The ID revealed that at least one of the perpetrators was an employee.

I asked that the employee be brought to the office to discuss the matter, but he had called in sick that day. So we reached him at his home and scheduled a meeting the following day. When he entered the meeting, his arm was completely bandaged, from his elbow to his fingers. He claimed that he had suffered an accident, but did not offer the details. Because of his injury, he had to keep the arm elevated. During our entire conversation, his arm was resting on the surface of the table and his hand was extended upward. The exchange went like this:

Us: You heard we had a break-in two days ago.
Him: Yes, awful.

Book 1 Leadership: The Responsibility to Ignite

Us: We are just talking to some employees who might have seen something.

Him: I didn't see anything.

Us: There was a great deal of blood. Evidently the person who is responsible got severely injured.

Him: Just awful.

Us: The person who we think might be involved dropped their wallet.

Him: Wow! Whose wallet was it?

Us: Yours.

Him: Damn it, I knew it was me.

I do not recall if we had him charged by the police, but as one might expect, we terminated his employment. For years afterward, "I knew it was me" became the phrase we used whenever there was a mistake!

In another incident, there was an associate who was involved in repeated human resources incidents. Simply stated, he did not "play well with others." He was regularly rude to his coworkers, was not trusted by his peers, and constantly tended to get caught up in office drama. At that point, I was only working at the subsidiary two days a month, so I had not met him yet. Evidently his performance was good, but the baggage he brought to work was completely unacceptable. Things had eroded to the point that his mother was regularly coming to the plant or calling in to advocate for her son. She had even been granted the opportunity to meet with his manager on several occasions.

I was furious. There had been months of complaints, and I requested that we terminate his employment. I think I might have even reminded the manager that we were not running a daycare center. However, the leadership dragged their feet and when I returned on

35

site after a time, I found he was still employed. And, he had continued to cause havoc. I ordered his immediate termination.

Within hours, his mother was at the plant causing quite a ruckus. Our HR lead begged me to meet with her; I agreed.

Expecting to be face-to-face with a 40-something helicopter mom, I was shocked when I was face to face with a woman who appeared to be in her 70s. Evidently, I had misunderstood the nature of the mom's involvement. She was not hostile or angry; rather, she seemed quite sad. She appealed to me to reinstate her son, but I had to refuse. The meeting ended peacefully.

Afterward, I met with the HR lead. I inquired how a woman so old could have a teenage son. As it turned out, the employee was... 43. I had wrongfully assumed we were dealing with a recent high school graduate. I guess some moms cannot allow their children to leave the nest.

As I flew home, I reflected upon the matter, finding it incredulous. A series of errors, along with a situation enabled by a weak manager (who evidently valued a warm body in a job over a healthy team), had crippled the operation.

The manager in question was later terminated. But you will meet him in an upcoming chapter.

CHAPTER 2

The Kindling That Optimizes Combustion

Before you are a leader, success is all about growing yourself. When you become a leader, success is all about growing others.

—Jack Welch

In my first book, *Unbundle It*, I referred to a leader as an orchestra conductor. It is a decade later and I have not discovered a better metaphor. A successful orchestra requires many elements to create the beautiful music that is appreciated by its audience. It's fair to say that making wonderful music that appeals to listeners is the orchestra's mission. Some of the most talented musicians are literally virtuosos of their specific instrument. The conductor leads the orchestra and understands what is required from each member of the team to create the optimized sound. The conductor has the unique ability to coordinate, even if he or she does not have the ability to play an individual instrument well enough on the stage. There are musicians who have the ability to become conductors, but in most cases they are much better suited to play their chosen instrument. Flutists play the flute, pianists the piano. Conductors... conduct.

In business, some of the best and brightest in the organization may not be able to lead effectively. Still others can only lead successfully at a specific level or in a specialized role. Other leaders might be very capable leading a specific company, while finding it a struggle to lead another. It is a matter of fit, culture, and values.

No person is great at every part of leading a team. The most mature leaders realize this, and surround themselves with other leaders who complement their skillset. If I tend to be an introvert and prefer to avoid the limelight, it's important that I find someone I trust who can be more outgoing.

Nevertheless, there are some attributes that most great leaders share. These attributes are the kindling that sustains the fire. Almost everyone would cite integrity as a keystone of great leadership, but the quality is not as simple as it might first appear. Being honest is one essential piece of the integrity puzzle, but it becomes a bit more complex as we peel the onion back.

There are times when the leader must be discerning. There are always situations where the leader is required to use discretion. But in some cases, using discretion could result in stakeholders questioning the integrity of the leader.

Examples of cases that might call for discretion would be legal matters, such as a merger or a divestiture. Another example might be a launch of a new product. Rumors will regularly circulate, and the leader – as the chief rumor crusher – must address the matter. It can be quite difficult to thread the needle of integrity without divulging information that could hurt the team.

Book 1 Leadership: The Responsibility to Ignite

Some leaders simply choose to lie – and then walk back the lies with excuses. That kind of behavior is contrary to the expected standard of excellence from leadership. A far better approach would be to carefully craft language that deflects from the core issue and, while probably vague, is factual.

It had been a well-circulated rumor that the company I led was seeking a change in control. I received a phone call from a business colleague; he asked me if my company had been purchased by another. I could have easily replied, "No comment," or "I cannot share details of our upcoming plans." For me at that time, it was easy to answer honestly; I was able to quell the rumor as inaccurate and say "no" to my colleague. A week later, we announced that we had purchased the other company in question.

The most difficult time for a leader might be when facing a crisis. Internally, he or she might be facing some rather difficult decisions. However, during such a crisis, it is essential that the leader remains stoic and reassuring to the team. One's integrity can be challenged in a crisis. The leader is conflicted with rallying the team and sharing vital news with them. In the most severe incidents, it might feel away from goodness not to share the facts with the team. But the leader's primary objective must be to cultivate hope within the team, until the leader cannot see any remaining pathway out of the crisis.

There is a fine line between lying to team members and encouraging them. There is a difference between not revealing all the details and fabricating a story. The idea is to keep the team members motivated through the crisis periods and not distract them.

A great example of an effective leader who decided not to reveal the full details of a crisis would be the beleaguered British prime minister, Winston Churchill, during the darkest days of World War II. He made passionate speeches that reassured the populace while knowing the circumstances were dire. Many historians believe that had Churchill not chosen the path he did, history might look significantly different.

Maintaining integrity during a crisis is a huge challenge for leaders. I have devoted a whole chapter of this book to crisis management. Employing the tactics explored in that chapter will go a long way to ensure that, as a leader, you will most likely never face those kinds of dire situations.

Maintaining a hard line when it comes to integrity requires great discipline. The temptation to take the easy route will be hard to resist. But discipline is often misunderstood as a punishment. While there is a time and a place for discipline, it is more important to motivate the team to push through. Much like an elite athlete, becoming a great leader takes commitment, resilience, and rigorous training. A leader must remain committed to the vision, without regard for his or her personal desires.

Discipline ensures that, at any given point, there will be consistency. Discipline is a mindset that sets an expectation within each member of the team. It is always doing what we say, and saying what we do. The leader models the discipline, sets the expectations, and ensures that each member of the team conducts himself or herself accordingly.

Great leaders have a healthy ego, but at the same time, it is controlled. They realize that they are the perfect person for the position. They expect to win. Nevertheless, they realize that winning is not about them or their personal success. The team must trump their own individual ambitions.

The leader must strike a very delicate balance, as success fuels the ego. It is easy for one's ego to become inflated. The temptation is real: *I am grateful* evolves into *I have earned it*. *I've earned it* becomes *I*

Book 1 Leadership: The Responsibility to Ignite

deserve it, and then cascades into *I must have it*. What is "it"? "It" can be any one of a countless number of unhealthy expectations.

It is a common occurrence for leaders to become punch-drunk on their success. They falsely come to believe that it is all about them, and that their brilliance is singular and irreplaceable. A good dose of humility must be inserted into this mindset. When the leader is in a position where there is no supervisory mechanism to counteract such impulses, disaster can occur. An executive coach, selected by the board of directors, is a good foil to stem such unhealthy behaviors.

The very greatest leaders make the decisions that they believe are best for the company even when those decisions can have a negative impact on them personally. The success of the enterprise must always prevail.

Committing to a culture where discipline is embedded is a bit like plowing fields and planting seeds that will grow. It is essential that we can share our story, and that requires adopting a culture where words matter, and communication – internally and externally – is thoughtful and purposeful.

Being a great communicator is a key element of becoming an exceptional leader. Communicating begins with learning to be a great listener. Not only is it important to listen, but it's important that your people understand that you have heard them.

Communication is so vital to the success of an enterprise that I devote all of Chapter 4 to examining the importance of a company's communication network. Communication is the number one factor cited by employees I've worked with as the single most important opportunity for improvement. Optimized communication adds clarity.

What follows is a collection of the attributes that are key to good leadership. There are 12, reminiscent of those life-altering 12-element programs that have unlocked so much life-changing goodness for millions. When we can release and master these dozen attributes, we will be equipped to ignite, fuel, and sustain fires – fires that will burn brightly long after we have left our leadership positions.

Humble

Humility is an often-overlooked and underappreciated attribute, because many see it as a quality not compatible with leadership. How can one be humble, yet lead a large organization? Is accepting a position in leadership, by definition, a bit prideful? Maybe, but being proud and being humble are not mutually exclusive. Quite the contrary – they can coexist and thrive, when employed properly.

A leader might be bursting with pride over a team victory, yet he or she can remain grateful that the team had been blessed to have had the opportunity. One can even be proud of some of his or her own accomplishments, but that kind of pride must be kept inside. Boastful statements tend to only be self-serving and will hurt the overall team morale.

Why is humility such a vital attribute? Humility creates connections with all team members at all levels in the organization. When one is truly grateful for all the team members and the work they do, it becomes rather easy to relate to them. I have always found it extremely exciting to visit with as many employees as possible, in various situations. Whether it's on the plant floor or at a softball game, creating a genuine connection is both uplifting and encouraging. I do not see it as a chore; rather, it is an imperative.

I absolutely love spending time with the employees on the plant floor. I find it refreshing and educational; I delight in hearing their stories. With frequent interaction over a period of time, you can develop a meaningful rapport. By listening and communicating, you will learn a great deal about what drives each team member. For their part, employees normally love this kind of outreach. As a result, their desire to help the company win is enhanced – and an intense loyalty is born.

One year, I was hosting a holiday party for just under 100 team members and their spouses. Because I had spent quality, interactive time with the employees, I knew something personal about each person. With information supplied by the HR department, I learned and memorized the name of each person's significant other.

As I greeted each team member at the party, I also welcomed their spouse by name. Moreover, I was able to weave a tidbit of personal information about the employee into the greeting. The response was overwhelming; I overheard a couple of the spouses raving about the fact that I knew everyone in the place. Most considered my knowledge miraculous, while my wife and I knew that it was much more about being truly interested rather than any wondrous talent I had.

Another time, I was responsible for bringing two groups of employees from different locations together to create a cohesive team. One group I had led for nearly five years; the other I had barely met. Priding myself on being a consummate showman, I decided that a rally was the best way to incorporate the team. As I recall, there were several hundred people in attendance. Since my original team would be required to move as part of the effort, less than 50 of the team members I already knew had been able to make the trip to the rally.

As the lights went down and the music rose, a large screen was illuminated. The name of each team member became visible and appeared to fly across the stage as "Simply The Best" blared throughout the theater. I was amazed as the small group who had made the trip were dancing to the music, while the much larger segment of the audience – the new team members – sat, rather stoically.

The rally lasted about two hours, with a half-dozen leaders speaking to the audience. Near the end of the rally, the demeanor in the crowd seemed to shift to being hopeful and more energized.

As I greeted the new team members afterward, one approached me. She seemed to be giddy. "I just started today, and when I saw my name on the screen, I couldn't believe it. I felt so special. How did you know?"

My answer was simple: "You are special to me, and it's my job to know."

I like to refer to these moments as being "real with the people." All know who the leader is. Associates are not buddies; they are key members of the team who are vital to the success of the enterprise. A leader should become vulnerable with the team members while maintaining his or her objectivity. That is the key.

When we get real with our people, really good things transpire.

Empathetic

An even rarer attribute in leaders is empathy. I have studied empathy as a phenomenon and discussed it with psychologists. They find that people with high empathetic scores on their personality tests are almost incapable of making tough decisions. An inability to make necessary, gut-wrenching decisions will render a leader ineffective.

During my career, I underwent a series of psychiatric tests. My empathy scores were extremely high. They were so elevated that the staff who administered the tests concluded that I might not be an effective leader. They mistakenly assumed that, if I was faced with a tough decision, I would not be able to act. Quite the contrary, though it was extremely difficult, I had no trouble making the calls I saw as essential for the long-term success of the overall team. In fact, I saw it as irresponsible to not make those calls. The greater good of the team must always be the primary consideration.

Some might have seen me as a bit cold-hearted, but when my decisions were examined over the course of time, it was generally agreed that the vast majority were correct. I may well have lost a dozen nights' sleep, but when the time came for action, I always tried to make the call I thought was best for the organization. Moreover, I tried to conduct myself with as little emotion as possible, and never asked a surrogate leader to take on the task of communicating unpleasant news. I saw it as my responsibility.

The idea of pushing tough decisions down to others on the team always seemed quite cowardly to me. However, on regular occasions, I did have to enlist other leaders to help answer questions and stamp out rumors when needed.

Empathy does not mean weakness. It's about care – and when we truly care for our team members, the feeling permeates throughout the entire organization.

Impartial

We all tend to gravitate to certain people in the workplace – and we find others more difficult to be with. It comes down to the idea of core values. Individuals that tend to share our values systems are – at least to us – more likable. We find it harder to spend time working with those who see things differently.

But a leader must not allow his or her personal preferences to creep into decision-making. If team members should suspect a leader of favoritism, trust is eroded, and the team suffers. Moreover, many leaders make the fatal error of socializing with certain select associates. When a leader and an employee become buddies, two critical risks emerge.

First, other employees see this FOB (friend of boss) situation as flagrant abuse and will often cite such a friendship as a source of strife in the organization. The second risk is even more debilitating. The leader unwittingly can lose his or her objectivity when the friend errors; it can become almost impossible to address the concern. When the FOB behavior is so severe that a termination is warranted, the situation becomes doubly difficult.

I made this type of error in judgment on a couple of occasions. In one case, because I was blinded by my friendship, I failed to realize just how debilitating the behavior had become.

Ultimately, the matter was addressed – the employee and the company agreed to part ways. Unfortunately, I waited so long to intercede that the company suffered almost irreparable damage. Worse yet, the employee's co-workers had been complaining about him for months, and I had no inkling about any of it. It was a harsh and expensive lesson for me of failure in leadership.

We must strike an extraordinarily difficult balance. We are drawn to reward those who are contributing to the success of the enterprise; yet, it is important that a leader has concrete proof that each employee to be rewarded is truly deserving.

The same is true when disciplining an employee. We can have a big problem with his or her performance or behavior, and that will result in a distaste for the individual. But a leader's like or dislike of a particular associate should play no role in the disciplinary process.

Impartiality might be the most difficult attribute for a leader to understand. It is almost universally agreed that it is a vital characteristic needed for leadership, but also that it is extremely hard to execute. It tends to be very subjective.

Curious

A great leader needs to be curious; we must consistently ask questions. It is natural for leaders to pose questions when the company is embroiled in a crisis or a significant failure. However, far too often, curiosity ends when the first cause is discovered. It is important to remember that the component that was discovered may only be a symptom or a part of what led to the unfavorable situation. Typically, the leader's curiosity is satiated with that initial discovery, and the company again goes about its business. But the organization may be destined to relive the negative incident because the issue may not have been properly vetted.

Something that surprises me is that many leaders never seem to be particularly curious when something great happens in their organizations. If we want these positive events to become repeatable and predictable, we should employ the same level of scrutiny to understand the causes for success as we do for failure.

Curiosity should also be directed outward. *What is my competition doing? Why are they doing that? What are the implications of the new governmental regulations?* The list of questions is nearly limitless. When we are curious, we are learning, and learning is an essential element of long-term success.

Educator

A desire for education grows out of curiosity. It involves a purposeful pursuit for knowledge. Every leader must become almost addicted to education; the thirst for knowledge should take on almost a cult-like devotion.

Great leaders should be avid readers. In my case, I am not a fan of reading. Still, I knew that through reading I could become enlightened to new ideas. Therefore, I forced myself to read on a regular basis.

I also made it a prerequisite that all leaders on my teams do some reading on an ongoing basis. I required team members to read books as a group and then meet to discuss what was learned.

The quest for knowledge must become hard-coded into the leader's persona. When the leader strives to gain as much knowledge as possible, and then ingrains that imperative into the psyche of team members, the entire team wins. But it is essential that the leader does not try to be the smartest person in the room. He or she should reserve that position for others on the team, while encouraging them to continue to feed that passion.

At the same time, a good leader must be willing to teach. He or she must employ the same level of intensity in being an educator as he or she was in becoming educated. Whether it is conducted in structured settings or during informal conversations, the desire to become educated and the willingness to educate others are vital parts of being a leader. In the arena of business, education is sometimes overshadowed by more pressing items, but a great leader cannot allow that to happen consistently.

Visionary

Great leaders are visionaries. They possess an uncanny ability to describe their vision with great clarity. They delight in creating a masterpiece and in sharing the details of that creation with their team. Everyone on the team clearly understands the **Why** of the leader's vision. The leader enlists a team of ambassadors who become equally passionate about the journey. When successful, the leader has instilled his or her passion within the team. A fire is ignited within each member – a fire that burns as brightly as the leader's.

The leader must be able to describe what success will look like in minute detail. When the vision is properly communicated, all of

Book 1 Leadership: The Responsibility to Ignite

the stakeholders – internal and external – will know exactly when the vision has been achieved. They will also know how they benefit from the success of the vision. When it is realized, the vision becomes the mission, and then a new, aspirational vision can be created and socialized.

One business that I ran was facing the real prospect of bankruptcy. We were sure that we were the best in the business, but we seemed unable to attract profitable prospective customers. So, the team was gathered; and in three days, we hammered out what we thought would be a five-year plan. Our vision became more of an awareness campaign. We stated the following mission and vision, and socialized them throughout the industry:

Mission: We are the Best Bakery in Pet
Vision: The Industry's First Choice for Baked Solutions

Within two years, our business was full. We had leapt the hurdles of potential insolvency. Amazingly, the bank that had threatened foreclosure began to urge us to take on debt. A few months later, we had secured a $6 million loan for capital expansion. Despite all the success, we continued to underperform; we were not reaching our true potential.

A new leader emerged, and I became her advisor. We decided that a new round of planning was required. As with the previous session, passion oozed throughout the planning process. We realized that our vision had become our mission. So, a new vision was born, and the result was impressive:

Mission: The Industry's First Choice for Baked Solutions
Vision: The Home of Unleashed Ideas Where We Say Yes to Success

Two interesting things came out of the planning sessions. First, we made the decision to create a test kitchen where our customers could create their own innovative products in a true factory environment. It was an amazing success, and it became fully booked almost immediately. In fact, a second shift was added to meet demand. We created an environment where lasting partnerships were fostered – and the innovations, once brought to market, all resulted in higher gross margins.

Within a year or two, the company was outperforming expectations financially, and all stakeholders were enriched by the fire that had been ignited and fueled. Celebrations that included the entire team swelled into amazing pep rallies. Indeed, the fire was burning brightly.

The other thing that materialized from those sessions became even more vital to the success of the organization. A new logo was born. Historically, we had used a logo that included clever imagery of a dog and cat superimposed upon each other. But it was, by all accounts, dull and uninspiring. Our new logo boasted a dog running, and its leash was left unused below its feet with the dog trampling it. The dot over the letter 'i' in our name became a tennis ball. Stakeholders loved the new logo. Something as simple as a logo became a game-changer.

I share this story for two reasons. First, because it was an amazing success – within five years, a company only days from bankruptcy developed into the leader in its category. Second, it is to demonstrate that the vision must transform your world. Fires can be lit, fueled, and sustained in a wide range of environments. Visionaries see fires burning where none exist, and they breathe in the oxygen vital to make the fires flourish.

Another word about that logo. Five years after I left that company, I met some of its leaders at a trade show. Upon spying the logo that I had come to love, I noticed a change. That tennis ball had become a globe. Immediately I knew that this next generation of leaders had stoked that company's fire with new fuel. "Global expansion?" I asked.

"We are bringing the world's passion for pets home," my longtime friend responded.

I reflected upon the brilliance, and realized that the fire set over a decade before was burning brightly. There is no greater reward for a leader than to witness the success of those who have followed.

Simplifier

Leaders are adept in finding simplicity in every complexity. In most cases, we find that there are just a few core root causes that are responsible for some of the most critical challenges. But those root causes might be enshrouded in a morass of "noise" that deafens our resolve. Timing and conflicting priorities can cloud a solution that lies right in front of us.

Early in my career, when I worked for the bakery, I realized the benefits of the ability to simplify. The company faced a true challenge. Each summer, the increase in demand for hot dog and hamburger buns far exceeded the bakery's ability to produce them. So, one year, in the months leading up to the summer, the leaders had decided to produce enough product to exceed the anticipated demand. The surplus buns were frozen and then thawed as needed.

Unfortunately, the experiment ended in disaster. The bakery did not have the infrastructure to physically move all of the thawed buns through the supply chain. Bringing the buns to the factory for distribution to the depots literally jammed the docks, overtaxed the transport equipment, and burdened the team members to the breaking point. Further, the disruption and confusion snarled the entire operation.

FIRESTARTER

After that debacle, the company still wanted to figure out how to produce and distribute enough buns for the summer, but without the chaos. The best minds in the company were assembled; as the new person on the team, I could see the situation with fresh eyes.

I offered a simple solution. Our records of product consumption gave us insight into how many buns would ultimately be shipped to each depot. So I proposed that we load the freezer by depot. When the time came for the buns' use, they could be transported directly to their destination. The idea was adopted, and it saved the company hundreds of thousands of dollars. It created a much safer environment for the workers, and allowed normal operations to flow during the high-demand period.

This is just one basic example of simplification in action. The puzzle was deemed too complex to solve, but that approach limited their thinking. They were far too invested in finding their way through the complexity to realize that a simpler solution was available – and easily addressable.

Challenges are simply mathematical equations. A one-variable problem is easily solvable. Two variables present a larger challenge, and only the brightest math minds can solve three- or four-variable equations.

In business, we see maybe a dozen or more variables that muddy a problem. To simplify, we hold as many variables constant as possible. At one business, I ran a complex inventory management system. Countless man-hours were invested to ensure its integrity, yet we continued to be plagued with surprise inventory outages. During one meeting, I noticed that the inventory on the report was odd. But my questions were met with disdain from those invested in the system.

I simply pointed out that the bin that contained the ingredient had a capacity of 100,000 pounds, but the inventory stated that we

Book 1 Leadership: The Responsibility to Ignite

had 200,000 pounds on hand. It was immediately agreed by all that there was a flaw in the logic of the system; the flaw was promptly discovered and corrected. Our inventory issues were solved.

Great leaders must become expert simplifiers. They must resist the temptation to migrate to complex solutions and instead examine the simple solutions first. Moreover, they must enlist others in adopting a similar mindset. A team that looks first to simplicity will more easily resolve the daunting issues facing a company. The simple solution unlocks time and enables organizational capacity to swell.

Teams adept in the art of simplification can accomplish more in less time than those who are not. Equally important, the tedious challenge becomes a riveting solution, and well-being soars.

> Perpetual optimism is a force multiplier.
> **– General Colin Powell**

Optimist

A great leader knows that optimism is contagious. The leader knows that if optimism can be managed properly, it can spread through the organization like wildfire. It can have a powerful impact on employee attitudes and behaviors. The company is represented by its brand, and mobilizing associates to become brand ambassadors is a vital component of success. Recruit the best and brightest throughout all levels in the company. Educate the associates on what makes the company great. Building enthusiasm for the brand leads to positive messaging.

A great example is the much-beleaguered Southwest Airlines. In recent years, the company seems to have lost its way. However, the airline was once known for operational excellence, and had a reputation as entertaining and exhilarating. At one point, customers flocked to the airline because they found a travel experience like no other. It was not just getting from point A to point B, it was the excitement of getting there on Southwest that made traveling singularly attractive. This was no accident; there was a purposeful brand ambassador program executed both internally and externally. The program was focused on promoting an image of good feelings and well-being. It was even widely reported that candidates who sought to join the Southwest team were required to tell a joke during job interviews. If the candidate was not funny, they simply did not make the cut.

Optimism escalates and becomes active cheerleading. I refer to this kind of effort as a Culture Warrior program. When properly implemented, the company will experience a groundswell of excitement, both internally and externally. Gone is the brand ambassador – in its place, a cadre of **brand evangelists** emerge. What is the difference? It's rather simple: an ambassador – after he or she is asked – will tell you something great about the organization. Or, the ambassador might weave a positive aspect about the company into a conversation with you. But a brand evangelist – without being asked – simply **must** share the news of the great things going on in the company. They cannot keep it to themselves, and will spread the good word to anyone who will listen.

As the evangelists trumpet the positive news, a reputation for excellence will permeate throughout the greater community. Often, the company will become well known for being a great place to work. That can become one of the best recruiting tools available to a company.

There are a few notable companies that are perennially recognized for being places where employees enjoy working. One is Wegmans, a

Book 1 Leadership: The Responsibility to Ignite

small yet growing grocery chain. It has been recognized by all who know it as an exceptional organization. It is a great place to work, a great place to shop, and a great place to be seen. Unscientific polling reveals that the average shopper spends more time and more money on each trip to Wegmans compared to peer competitors. It has become a true destination. Wegmans attracts the most desirable team members – and customers – through their purposeful program.

At one point in my career, I was recruiting a very talented person for a key leadership position. As a final push to sign her, I reminded her that we had a Wegmans near our town. She turned down the job, but in her rejection letter, she wrote that she almost accepted due to Wegmans being nearby. Clearly, Wegmans has created an enticing brand.

None of this brand strength is possible unless the organization's leadership buys in to building it. Equally important, when leadership changes, the corporate culture can erode if it is not nurtured. Negligence can lead to a tarnished image. I find it fascinating that many successful companies – the ones that create megabrands – fail to invest in what might be the most important brand of all, their overall company brand. The company brand is the one that deserves purposeful investment and nurturing.

Think about those companies whose names are synonymous with preeminence in their fields. Most companies do not excel in all areas, but many are known for particular areas of expertise. When we think about Amazon, we immediately are drawn to what will be an efficient and all-encompassing shopping experience. However, Amazon was historically tarnished with the reputation of being a very poor place to work. Fast-forward a few years to the present, and we see Amazon investing in a multimillion-dollar advertising campaign, attempting to convince the public and prospective employees that they are a great workplace. But if they had recognized their errant approach years ago, Amazon could have avoided the entire debacle.

At the same time, there are companies that experience drastic declines. That phenomenon is nearly always associated with a change in leadership. The new leader either does not fit the corporate culture, or refuses to promote it.

Then, there are companies that rise to prominence after decades of mediocracy. A great example is Yuengling. It is the oldest brewery in the United States. When I was a 20-something, Yuengling beer was known as inexpensive and ordinary. In the past 20 years, the brand has undergone a metamorphosis – becoming one of the most respected, highly desirable brews in the industry. What happened? One can be sure that a leadership change, or a leader-inspired strategic shift, ignited such a fiery blaze of brand growth.

Coach

"Coach" is not a term that was broadly used until recently. When I started my career, the term "coach" was applied only to a person who guided a sports team. But over the decades, life coaches, career coaches, and team coaches have become rather ubiquitous.

Great leaders learn to develop themselves into exceptional coaches. As the term suggests, the coach will encourage team members when they are down. A coach will promote and reward correct behaviors, and help keep team members grounded. It's a constant balance between reinforcement and redirection. It is about being fluid, working behind the scenes.

When I was a young leader developing my style, I had set a goal for myself and my team – to score a 900 on an American Institute of Baking sanitation audit. My team worked smartly and tirelessly.

The audit was unannounced and when the inspector arrived, it was all hands on deck. The team executed flawlessly, and the audit was proceeding smoothly. As we headed for the close-out meeting after three arduous days, I was convinced that we had achieved our goal.

As background, the facility had failed the audit the year before, scoring below 600. The 900 level was the gold standard, reserved for only the top 1 percent of food facilities. Platitudes were piled on us by the inspector... and the final score was 895. Visibly shaken, I asked for an explanation.

"I cannot in good conscience score a facility 900 when they failed the previous year. I cannot and will not do it," he answered.

A devastated and defeated Elliott Haverlack walked out of the meeting and readied himself for the long ride home. A year of effort and two 16-hour days had left me mentally and physically drained. I think I was sadder for the team than I was for myself. They too had made one hell of an investment.

My manager found me in my office and insisted that we go to a local tavern and celebrate. He encouraged me, beyond anything I imagined possible. "The entire company is going to be so proud of this feat," he started. I do not recall much else he said, until he decided to change tactics a bit.

During the intense two-day audit, the inspector had not seen a single bug. The building was five stories tall, plus a basement, and was over 100 years old – so naturally, there were bugs or pests that harbored in some cracks and crevices. But we had them under control. Nevertheless, at one point during the investigation, the inspector had roused one of those bugs and it crawled between his legs. I had casually stepped on it and slid my foot across the floor, thinking no one had seen.

"What do you think our score would have been if the inspector had seen that bug that you stepped on during the inspection?" my manager asked.

His statement and the one that followed have stayed with me these nearly two score years.

"The last time I was in this place, I was with my girlfriend and my ex-wife, and my current wife walked in. If you are ever having a bad day, think about how that went down," he counseled.

It was my first official coaching experience and he had done a masterful job. He opened my eyes to perspective. With perspective, I was able to rally my team and help coach them through the disappointment. And I was better able to equip them to leap the hurdles that lay ahead.

As for my boss, I suspect that he might have scored slightly low on the integrity scale. But we scored 900 on the next audit, and along with that came a promotion.

When a team member is struggling, the coach will coach them up or coach them out. Coaching a team member out of the organization – when done properly – is beneficial to all involved, even to the person who is asked to leave. In most cases, it comes down to a matter of fit.

In the final assessment, the coach will enrich the journey and enhance the performance of the team. Almost all of the attributes reviewed in this chapter are embodied in a good coach.

Great leaders who have evolved into great coaches also recognize that it is equally important to find a coach to help them with their own development. We all have strengths and weaknesses. Some of our most severe weaknesses can morph into blind spots. We may exhibit behaviors that are repellent to others, yet we fail to see any problem. A good coach will help us move past those blind spots.

Leadership positions can be quite lonely. The right external coach can become an essential confidant, allowing the leader to openly share their deepest thoughts. By doing so, the leader can validate mission-critical decisions in a confidential environment.

Courageous

Leaders must be courageous. That does not mean that a leader is a superhero who dramatically flies in to save the day. Courage means always doing the right thing, even when – and especially when – it is hard. And it will usually be hard. That is why not everyone is cut out to be a leader.

There are many people who know the right thing to do, but they find it too difficult. So, they opt for the easy way out.

Assuming that you have a good dose of humility in your psyche, you will probably not realize the status you hold in the eyes of the broader team. I refer to the effect of the leader's status as "coattails," and the coattails of the leader have vast implications throughout the enterprise.

You, the leader, might still see yourself as that junior associate who was wide-eyed and hungering to achieve. But in the team's eyes, you hold the preeminent position. Your words and your actions matter. Courage is a game-changer. You and your team will be rewarded for your courage.

Risk-Taker

Managing risk is an essential element of leadership. Great leaders know that risk-taking is part of every successful endeavor. Jack Welch, former chairman and CEO of General Electric, described it as "going with your gut" or "being able to see around corners." Great leaders are not afraid to "go with their guts." They have an uncanny way of predicting outcomes. When they are wrong, they have the integrity to admit their mistakes; but also the courage to plot a new course, the discipline to see things through, and the curiosity to learn from the experiences.

One leader I worked with was absolutely terrified of taking on any risk. He would counsel me during decision-making by stating, "But there is risk." I would rebut his concerns; yet, he would repeat the same line over and over. One day, I asked him how he managed the risk of driving to work. He was so terrified of the phantom risks he saw as threats at work that he failed to see that we all manage risks in almost every activity.

There is simply no way to remove all risk from a business setting. The question becomes: How much risk are we willing to take? Leaders who are risk-averse tend to create dull and boring cultures. On the other hand, big risk-takers can be seen as reckless and irresponsible. A good leader finds the balance, knowing there will be many successes and some failures.

Steadfast

Temptation is something that will creep into your decision-making on a regular basis. It seems like it is almost always there, urging you to take the easy path or to make the convenient choice. It can be a real struggle. When temptation rears its ugly head, we must be ready to crush those impulses. A visual reminder can be a constructive helper in winning that battle. My reminders were always on my desk – a picture of my wife and one of each of my children. They were positioned in a way that only I could see their smiling faces. But more importantly, they were always watching me. When faced with a tough decision, I simply looked into their eyes and asked myself: Would they be proud of the decision I am about to make? Those pictures have been a powerful motivator for most of my career. I am certain that I made many tough, yet just, decisions through their influence. I've since added my granddaughter into the array. Her innocence shines out of the photo – it is extraordinarily reassuring, and has become my final arbiter for decisions.

Burn Brighter

Great leaders will have a vision, and they will share that vision both internally and externally. They will set a course to make that vision a reality. They will gather the right team members, map the perfect strategy, and execute with sound tactics.

Great leaders remember to be thankful and grateful. "Thankful" is an outward gesture to reward others through words and deeds. "Grateful" is more internalized – we realize that we have accomplished our vision, but we also recognize that success contains an element of fortunate circumstance.

Great leaders strive to be part of a more capable tomorrow. When mistakes are made or character flaws emerge, great leaders learn from them, and move on. Embracing our failures might even be more important than celebrating our successes.

Lighthearted Lessons: Unintended, Yet Educational

During my time presiding over the family business I mentioned, I met interesting people and had some rather memorable experiences. One remarkable character was my boss. In many ways, he was the best boss I ever had; he was a very capable and effective person. However, he sometimes did miss the mark.

We had a very open relationship and we shared a myriad of personal topics with each other. At one point, I told him that the other leaders needed to hear from him. The team had recently accomplished some great things, and the employees were desperate for some well-earned praise.

"You do that all the time," he offered. "Why do I have to do it?"

"Because you own the place, and it just means more coming from you," I countered.

A few days later, he addressed the key leadership team. "Elliott tells me that you want to hear from me more often." He added, "Please consider my silence as high praise."

Not exactly what I was looking for, but it made for a great chuckle.

The rally I described in this chapter had its own rather funny moments. Now, almost 25 years later, one stands out. I had been blessed with an extraordinarily talented and dedicated assistant. She had been the creator of the visual and audio extravaganza for the rally. Considering the technological limitations of the day, it was a bit of a marvel. Since I was relocating, I had been assigned a new laptop; but since I was in transition, I often had my old one with me too. Laptops of that era were extremely heavy and bulky.

My assistant insisted that she keep the laptop that contained the presentation with her until the show concluded. That meant she would have to transport it with her from her home city to the event venue. At nearly 100 pounds, it took a rather unwieldy effort for her to schlep it onto the plane.

After the successful rally and an enjoyable reception, she and others were preparing to return home. Watching her struggle with the laptop, I insisted that she just return it to me. I also made her promise to take the rest of the day off as a reward for having pulled off such an amazing feat.

Later at the office, I was involved in a conversation with two female employees. I unpacked the laptop and a ball of material popped out.

Genuinely surprised, I questioned, "What is that?"

"Looks like pantyhose to me," one associate answered.

Without thinking, I instinctually uttered, "Oh… they must be my assistant's."

The expression on both women's faces was most disquieting as I realized what they were probably thinking. Quickly, I went into explanation mode. Because I was so unprepared, I stuttered and stammered.

A short time later, I called my assistant. "Did you by chance leave something in my laptop bag?" I asked.

Knowing exactly what I had found, she shouted, "Oh my gosh. I am so embarrassed."

"Try having them pop out in front of two female employees who really do not know me well," I answered.

The entire episode was so innocent that I could not even be angry. She had torn her pantyhose while deplaning and decided to change them in an airport bathroom.

I never knew if those two employees ever truly believed me, but since my response was so genuine, I think – I hope – they gave me the benefit of the doubt.

CHAPTER 3

Sourcing the Elements for Combustion

Great things in business are never done by one person;
they're done by a team of people.

– Steve Jobs

There is quite a bit packed into the previous chapter. You might think that you possess all of the leader attributes outlined. But to many, it might feel like a daunting task – maybe even an unachievable one – to combine all of those attributes. Likely, it is not possible for one individual to embody all the traits of a good leader.

Good news – you do not have to be great at all of those things. Remember – you are the conductor; you just need to find other leaders who will complement your style. If you do not see yourself as a cheerleader, then hire a few energetic souls who are so inclined. If they bring pompoms to the job interview… so much the better.

Still, there will be others that read the previous chapter and see themselves as experts who have all the attributes in abundance. To be real, such people would most likely be suffering from a severe lack of self-awareness, and would have no business leading any team. Further, it would be fair to suggest that they might be lacking in the first attribute – humility.

Every leader must understand that a unique amalgamation of people, processes, and priorities is required for any business to survive. Moreover, it is each leader's responsibility to optimize all of those factors to ensure that the organization thrives at the highest level. Each end-result will be unique, and constant adjustments are simply part of each journey. Just like a fire that needs to be stoked and tended, the team will need to be continually monitored and encouraged to keep it at peak performance.

It may sound like a daunting task. But as the leader develops, these imperatives become embedded into his or her mindset. And then, due to successful leadership, they spread throughout the entire enterprise. More great news – there is a road map available. While it is adaptable, the overall principles will guide the journey to excellence. Many of these wayfinders are discussed in the pages that follow.

We can learn a great deal about an emerging leader's character through his or her focus on the intangibles. Culture is the quintessential intangible that is often overlooked or underexplored by immature leaders – or by leaders who might best seek another profession. A failure to focus enough on culture usually creates a toxic work environment. Then, dissatisfaction runs rampant.

Culture

Culture is vitally important. Understanding the implications of cultural differences, and focusing on aligning the culture with the team (and the business) is paramount. A great leader might become ineffective when put into a position where the existing culture does not mesh with the leader's style. Do we change the leader or do we change the culture? It is difficult to answer that, but when the culture is in conflict with the leadership, change must occur.

On the surface, it seems more expedient to change the leader, but that could be exactly the wrong approach. The business might already suffer from a culture of toxicity. Or perhaps the leader does not invest enough time into understanding the culture. If a leader fails to fully grasp, and align with, the optimal values of the company, the company will most assuredly underperform over time.

Every fire requires specific ingredients in order for it to ignite and blaze. Oxygen is the invisible ingredient required for any fire, and culture is the oxygen of business. If the culture is tainted or nonexistent, even the most talented igniter will fail.

Steve Jobs of Apple might go down in history as one of the most brilliant, yet misunderstood leaders of his day. Like all leaders, he had plenty of blind spots. In many circles, he was known to be manipulative, mean-spirited, cold, and even unethical. His inability to see his flaws and correct them led to his undoing.

Founded on April 1, 1976, by Jobs and Steve Wozniak, Apple became a cultural phenomenon. By 1983, Apple had joined the Fortune 500 – at the time, the fastest company to ever do so. But by 1985, the board of directors decided that a change was necessary. Jobs's services were no longer required – or so they thought.

Apple did well after that for a short while, but by 1996, the company was facing some significant challenges. Jobs was reengaged, and the rest is history. Apple was the first company to surpass a market cap of $1 trillion. Then it was the first to exceed $2 trillion in market cap – and most recently, it exceeded $3 trillion. There is no question that Apple is on fire.

Nevertheless, the Apple story reveals that some of the best and brightest are not good fits for the culture. John Sculley, a very successful businessman, had joined Apple at the prodding of Jobs, and eventually aided in Jobs's ouster. Under Sculley's leadership of Apple, it can be reasonably stated that the company suffered; it posted disappointing financial results. In my view, Sculley literally cut into the core of the Apple phenomenon and attempted to reinvent the company. He was forced to resign in 1993.

Some would say that Sculley performed admirably. I would respectfully offer that much of his early success was due to innovations that were in the pipeline before his ascension. I would further assert that Sculley's leadership style created the environment that led to the decline of Apple during his reign.

In many cases, it can take years for the outsider to recognize that a poisonous culture has infected a business. In my view, Apple under Sculley is a textbook example of how a leader trampled on a unique and entrepreneurial culture and attempted to fit it into a corporate playbook. A seasoned leader who had been successful with another company attempted to replicate that success by forcing the new entity into a preordained cultural box. The results were disastrous.

Was Jobs the firestarter? I think so. I suppose we may never know all the details of the rise, fall, and rebirth of Apple, but Jobs ignited an inextinguishable fire in the company that has become unquenchable. And it appears to be intensifying as we herald in a new generation.

Leadership matters. Top leadership changes have a profound impact on the performance of the company. Just because someone is a great leader or has a good pedigree does not mean that he or she is the right person for the job. General Electric is a great example. Led by Jack Welch for 20 years, the company was considered unstoppable.

After Welch retired, the company appointed hand-picked successors – but the company declined and would not recover.

At the same time, there are true success stories where a change in leadership was instrumental in a corporate turnaround. In 2000, A.G. Lafley's ascension to lead Procter & Gamble was a game-changer. The results are well-documented.

Shared Values

There are a few vital elements to be considered when building one's team. The most important thing is finding people who share your values. It is commonly referred to as "fit." Ethics might be one of the more subjective and difficult concepts to reconcile among different people. What might be considered completely acceptable to one person might be viewed as abhorrent or unconscionable to another.

A good example of such a situation comes from this past year in my personal life. The lottery jackpot had swollen to over $1 billion. I was visiting with one of my friends, and advised him that I was going to grab some tickets on my way home. The look on his face was one of total shock.

"Please do not tell me you are a gambler," he said, and added, "That's sinful."

"Have you ever thought about all the people I will be able to help if I win?" I answered. His demeanor completely changed, and the next time I saw him, he asked me if I had won anything.

In the business world, conflicting viewpoints and values are usually more subtle, but no less troubling if left unresolved. Understanding your value system and the value systems of your team members is an essential element in team success.

If you make it a priority, sourcing team members who share your values is a straightforward task. Far too often, values are overlooked, with candidates more often evaluated on intelligence and experience. Certainly, both experience and intellect are important factors in the selection process, but when they are allowed to muddy an obvious disconnect in values, it is a critical error in judgment.

Personality Types

In addition to shared values, there is another valuable element that is often overlooked by leadership: personality type. One's value system is different from one's personality type. Far too often, we blur the lines between the two. In personality typing, we are looking to recruit individuals for the team who fall into a variety of categories.

I am a student of the Myers-Briggs personality type format. In Myers-Briggs, there are 16 identified personality types. After careful study, I found that my best teams formed when we sourced leaders from as many of the personality types as possible.

Equally important, when we educate team members on the type differences – and help them understand the pitfalls of their type – we take a big step toward cooperation. Gone are the struggles that lead to dysfunction; instead, we experience productive outcomes.

I am an ESTP (Extrovert Sensing Thinking Perceiving), and as such, I am prone to act first and ask questions later. Knowing that about myself, I can purposefully control my impulses. I know that I need to ask more questions and gain more input before acting.

Conversely, my INFJ (Introvert Intuitive Feeling Judging) co-worker isn't trying to throw roadblocks up just to annoy me. But they might see me as reckless, and understandably try to stop what they see as a potential disaster.

When I first became enamored with the personality type concept, I was leading a team of very talented individuals. Together we accomplished great things, but we seemed to regularly miss deadlines on projects and tasks, and took very few notes. We were generally late for meetings, and we spent a great deal of time cleaning up messes.

After the team was tested, we learned that every member was a P, or a perceiving personality preference. We immediately modified our approach and forced ourselves to be more disciplined. It was quite a struggle, because we were all predisposed not to value such structure.

The next three leadership hires were purposely recruited for having J, or Judging, preferences. Including those personality preferences enhanced the team's success. The added competitive spirit of the J people inspired each team member to ramp up their performance, despite their personal preferences.

Adopting a culture where personality preferences are socialized and embraced does require that team members have some discipline and mental maturity. Some will attempt to use their personality type as a crutch or an excuse for bad behavior. Others will attempt to assert that their personality type is superior. In the worst scenario, a candidate might perceive a certain personality type as desirable, and then attempt to trick the testing to become that type. People of that ilk have no business remaining on a team, and they should be coached out.

Still, when teams get the combination of values and personality types right, it is extremely powerful. Shared values plus differing personality types is a winning combination.

Filling the Seats in the Orchestra Pit

You are like the conductor in an orchestra. Once you are equipped with a set of core values that the company can embrace, you can commence finding team members who will fit. The first thing we want to do with a candidate is review the resume. During the review, we are not looking for experience or achievements – although those factors are important. We are searching for style. We ask ourselves: Is this a resume that seems to have been written by a person who shares our values? Some red flags to look for are overly self-serving language or buzzwords.

A resume is nothing more than a promotional page. It's a bit of a paradox – it is the quintessential example of self-promotion; but in that promotion, we learn a great deal about the candidate.

If the resume contains explicit details, we can surmise that the individual values results and might have a tendency to micromanage. If the resume is vague, it will imply something completely different. If it includes statements that seem to be self-serving, it can reveal a bit about their ego. Words like "led" and "managed" pop up in resumes regularly. Are you looking for a manager or a leader?

A few years back, my company was looking for a chief operating officer, or COO. This was a key position; a person to fill the role was desperately needed.

A resume was sent over for my review, but I immediately advised the company to pass. It was clear from the resume's content that the candidate had a mountain of experience and was exceptionally intelligent. It also appeared to me that he would not be a good fit. Two words that came to my mind after my review were "bureaucratic" and "corporate." Since we were a more entrepreneurial and hands-on organization, I feared a cultural misalignment.

Nevertheless, others on the team felt I had been too quick to disqualify him. So, we brought him in for an in-person interview. He wowed all of us. It was ultimately my decision, and I jumped at the chance to get him on board. I opted to skip the personality testing that I preferred to be part of the process. I am an ESTP, as you might recall.

Our new COO was bright and charming and one of the more intellectual people I had ever encountered. He impressed us for a few months... and then that whole fit and values thing reared its ugly head. His employment was eventually terminated.

His resume had spoken volumes about the person he was. It turned out that he conducted himself exactly as his resume predicted he would. But he had charmed the socks off of us during the interview process. The person we interviewed was a figment of our infatuation.

It's important to note that this person could have been a top-tier leader in a different organization. Talented and brilliant, he brought a great deal to the enterprise. His attributes were just not enough to overcome the disastrous mismatch of values. His story is one of the most significant hiring failures in my career.

During an interview, to get an idea of the person's values and style, we want to probe with questions that have nothing to do with experience or intellect. We will ask questions like, "Think of a person you admire; what is it about them that makes you feel as you do?"

Another good question might be, "Tell me about your greatest accomplishment in life." If they answer with a story about something in their career, probe further by asking about a personal triumph. Such a question often throws socially immature people off their game. Since there are no right or wrong answers, questions like these tend to get to the heart of a person's value system.

It is also often helpful to inquire about a defeat or setback they have experienced. More immature candidates often are unable to answer that question. Others might be quick-witted enough to create what I refer to as a failure shrouded in a triumph. "I found myself working too hard, and was completely exhausted when I successfully completed the assignment," might be an example of that type of answer.

After reviewing and approving the resume, the next step should be a quick internet check. A background check, coupled with an internet search, is an essential part of the hiring process. In some cases, a background lookup can save a significant amount of time and effort in examining a candidate. It might not be easily accomplished – candidates with common names might yield so many search results that there is little value. Despite that possibility, the keystrokes required are a worthy investment.

Almost every rule has exceptions, and sometimes during hiring we find that we might need to break our own rules. At one point in my career, I was faced with a rather difficult HR decision. The company was in desperate need of an experienced operator to lead our manufacturing function. A candidate emerged who possessed the skills and experience, but it seemed like he was completely misaligned with our values.

Realizing that he would likely not make the grade in the long term, I hired him anyway. Frankly, he did great work and lifted us operationally to levels previously not possible. And we gave him every opportunity to advance his values to match those that the team embraced. But ultimately, I had to terminate his employment. Despite hours of coaching, he simply could not – or would not – change.

In the final assessment, the company was far better off for having had him in the manufacturing leader role for over two years. Unlike the previous example I mentioned, I found that this particular hiring decision – while not optimal – was exactly what the company needed for a time. The episode led me to realize that, when faced with no perfect solution, one must find the least imperfect one.

Another great lesson for me came from an exchange with that brilliant leader that I introduced in Chapter 1. She and I were searching for a head of operations. She had learned that a longtime industry veteran was exploring ways to move to the geographic area where our company was located. He was from that area originally, and would have been the kind of teammate that almost anyone in a peer company would have sought out. There was one problem: the scale of our company could not support the cost of such an overqualified candidate.

But we found that because he was nearing the end of his career, he was looking to slow down a bit. He was looking to return home, and really wanted to be part of a winning team. As such, he was willing to take a bit less in cash compensation. Still, the gap between what we could offer and what he desired was significant.

This woman, my associate, was rather insistent that we land the veteran candidate. Finally, I advised her that we could not afford to pay him. We could not risk the incongruent pay disparity with the other leaders. In fact, his minimum salary request was significantly higher than her own compensation package.

"I've discussed this with the other leaders and we really want him," she said, and added, "As for me, doesn't a great NFL coach pay the star quarterback more than himself?"

I had never thought about it in that way. We hired him; he was the classic "missing piece of the puzzle" and a perfect cultural fit. The company grew to such a scale that we were able, over time, to increase the pay rates for the other leaders. This was a great lesson for me in choosing team over self. Interestingly, as a result of our hire, all stakeholders were rewarded. And when it came my time to make a similar decision at a different company, the answer was already burning within my psyche.

The Assistant

One of the most vital positions in the organization is that of the assistant. While technically not a leader by title, the same attributes that define a great leader can be found in an exceptional assistant. Far too often, the role of the assistant is underappreciated by leaders. The leader wrongly assumes that the assistant's primary role includes those traditional secretarial duties such as typing, filing, and answering the phone. While those activities are important, they are not as significant as the more essential elements of what makes a great assistant.

A great assistant is an extension of the leader. They become an ambassador for the leader and the company. They embody optimism and add a brightness to the organization that is extremely powerful.

Assistants can also be the "canary in the cage," a term from the mining days. Because they are so well connected with the team, they can help the leader navigate the possible pitfalls of new programs, continuing vital initiatives, and difficult periods.

Assistants also serve as chief rumor crushers. They can stop those carcinomas before they metastasize. Also, in their role of cheerleader, they can champion initiatives when required.

During my career, I have been blessed to have three amazing assistants. Each brought a valuable perspective and enhanced the corporate culture through their actions and their personas. One in particular, who worked with me for over a decade, was unflappable. She lit up every room that she entered, and never had a bad day. Or, at the least, she was very good at keeping her misgivings private.

At one time during my career, I reported to a man who was considered a scourge; most people feared him. His assistant was an absolute terror and she exacerbated his reputation. To be sure, the guy had a rather crusty persona, but he was not nearly as bad as his reputation. Once I was able to develop a relationship with him, I found him to be far more reasonable than most others thought.

I decided to advise him that his assistant was hurting him. He laughed it off. There was something really evil about her, but he was blind to it. I do not believe that his unwillingness to address the issue had anything to do with a misplaced loyalty to her; rather, he just did not want to deal with making a change.

Not surprisingly, it was soon confirmed that her outward persona mirrored a truly diabolical inner spirit. The boss was forced to terminate the assistant's employment after it was discovered that she was using his company credit card to pay her personal expenses. The total was over $20,000. Worse yet, the company viewed his failure to catch the theft as negligence on his part. He was told that he would be responsible for repayment. From my perspective, the $20,000 was peanuts, compared to the ill will she created and spread.

After much coaching, I was able to convince him to evaluate the assistant role through a different lens and hire someone with different qualities. He then selected a delightful assistant, and she helped to vastly improve his image. He still had his idiosyncrasies, but she was a master at mitigating them. It was an amazing, game-changing point in his career.

It is important that the leader keep things in perspective. He or she should realize that with the job of assistant comes incredible power. Confidentiality between leader and assistant is a must. Just remember that as a leader, all eyes are on you and your relationship with this person.

FIRESTARTER

We Have a New Team Member – Now What?

In human resources today we hear about onboarding, which used to be known as orientation. But onboarding sounds cooler and fresher, so we will use that term.

We should have a formal onboarding plan written specifically for each new hire. Although onboarding plans will be unique for each individual, every plan will include common elements. And, part of the onboarding process should include two often-overlooked elements.

First, each new hire should be assigned an onboarding partner or advocate. The advocate should be a trusted member of the team who will help guide the new person through the orientation process. The partner will get to know the new hire on a personal basis; they will not just be co-workers.

The advocate's role is to answer questions and offer suggestions. The advocate also will be trained to listen for fresh thinking or ideas. He or she might even probe for information. The advocate can ask the newcomer questions, like: "How have you seen this done before?" Or, "We are having this problem; have you ever faced a similar one?"

The first day on the job is special. The new employee has no company dogma that will cloud his or her perception. If not properly onboarded, by day two they will already start to perceive and accept some of the barriers that the company has unwittingly placed on itself. Without being fully aware, the new hire will start to "fall in line." Ideally, the advocate will encourage any challenges to the status quo from the new associate.

Here is a story to illustrate my points. On my first day on an assignment, I entered a factory and was given a Tyvek smock to wear. I questioned its use but was advised that the law required it. I knew that was an inaccurate statement; I pressed further. I was then told that it was an industry requirement. Again, I was aware that that, too, was incorrect.

In addition to adding cost to the operation, the smocks were uncomfortable. They made an already hot environment even more miserable.

The next time I visited the factory, the smocks were not required. I realized that my insistence that the smocks were an unnecessary expense might have helped the company dig a bit deeper for information. They discovered that I had been correct.

I have a more significant example of a new associate making an impact. A very important customer mandated that we add a cumbersome and expensive step to our shipping process. It was nearly impossible to execute, and we struggled mightily. But during an onboarding process with a new associate, he advised me that his previous employer had simply refused to comply with such a demand, and the customer had agreed. We followed suit, and there were no repercussions.

Another vital, often overlooked part of the onboarding process is observation. New leaders should be exposed to most – if not all – of the departments in the enterprise, so they can see those areas. When I was in the pet nutrition industry, I found that sales leaders and marketing leaders tended to recoil a bit when their onboarding process had them spend a few hours in a place such as a meat room, but they did gain an important perspective.

Meat rooms tend to be hot and wet, and the aroma is intense. Dogs and cats seem to thrive on meat-based diets; therefore, it is a requirement to properly include meat in the product. Leaders who saw – and smelled the meat – had a better idea of what the workers were accomplishing. Often, leaders outside the operations orbit do not understand the commitment required by all employees to create the products they are peddling.

At one company I joined, a veteran sales lead had never entered the factory. One day, I asked him to join me on a see-it-all tour. After that day, every time the team discussed rewards and recognition, he would be the biggest advocate for the members who worked in the plant. Clearly, prior to his in-person tour, he had no idea what it took to make the products he sold.

Focusing on Trust

To realize an optimized team performance, a significant and ongoing investment is required. Moreover, a genuine buy-in from the top of the organization is vital.

The most overarching imperative is to build trust within the leadership team. Without trust, almost nothing productive is possible from a team. When we do not trust, we are likely to question the motivations of others. It is particularly debilitating when distrust leads to disagreement.

Focusing on trust requires us to get to know our teammates on a very personal level. When we share struggles and triumphs on a personal basis, we become much more vulnerable. As we build a foundation based on trust, perceptions that could lead to misconceptions evolve into understanding and acceptance. We learn that our teammates are not intentionally trying to create more work or difficulties. They might have differing perspectives but still genuinely want what is best for the organization. Moreover, we should remember that their struggles outside the workplace might be affecting their demeanor. They are our colleagues, and deserving of our understanding – not our ire.

We should realize that we are all on our own journeys. Teammates are trying to achieve some disparate goals and some that are held in common. One team member might be individually focusing on becoming a black belt in karate; but all team members are working to secure a brighter future for themselves and their families. Throughout their journeys, team success is vital to them achieving their goals.

Formal training sessions that focus on key elements are essential. In particular, sessions should include examining personality types. I mention that topic because I see it as extraordinarily important. I do not believe that exploring the various personality types is usually done to a level where the organization realizes the full benefits.

Once we have a healthy team functioning at a high level, we can add tools to help enhance the journey. Effective meetings, conflict resolution, and even handling difficult conversations are but three great examples of topics to be explored through formal training sessions.

Off-site meetings are an important part of team-building. They should be "cellphones and computers off" sessions. However, those requirements are very hard to administer. A leader must be disciplined and have enough courage to counter the expected pushback from team members.

The Stages of Competence

In business, and in life, there are four stages on the path to competency. These principles transcend everything we do.

The first stage is unconscious incompetency. Simply stated, we are unaware that we want to learn something, and so we are not proficient.

The second stage is conscious incompetency. We want to do something, but just are not skilled enough yet.

The third stage is conscious competency. We are able to successfully accomplish the mission, but we have to think about our every action.

The final stage in unconscious competency. We are proficient and we do not even have to think about it.

Think about driving a car. At first, we do not think about it... and we certainly have no skills. One day, we decide that we would like to learn, but it is a real struggle. Next, we pass our test, but we are very purposeful in each action behind the wheel. Then, one day, we hop in the car and are down the road without a thought.

The problem in business is that the leadership often is not driven to push the team through the frustration of moving from stage three to stage four. They invest significant resources and time introducing a concept and training the team, only to get frustrated when the team cannot perform competently without a lot of thought and effort. Can you imagine how many people would be unable to drive if they had simply given up when things got difficult?

In addition to an incredible waste of time and resources in training, the team tends to lose confidence in the commitment of the company. In the most severe cases, the team's mindset becomes one of endurance. They have experienced these types of training programs before, and are all too willing to wait it out until the leaders get bored and move on to the next greatest program that they read about in an article or hear about at a conference. Employees are more observant than we might think, and they will begin to question why resources are wasted so flagrantly.

Book 1 Leadership: The Responsibility to Ignite

The Limitation of Time

Throughout my 40-plus-year career, I have learned that the clock stops for no person and no priority. Time is constant and cannot be changed or manipulated. We ponder, we question, we panic... and time marches on, unaffected by our strife. We can, however, become proficient in using time, and therefore become its master.

My epiphany regarding time came nearly 20 years ago. As part of a developmental program, I was urged to work from home one day a week. I discovered that I was able to complete much of my daily tasks at a breakneck pace, finishing early. I was also able to participate in meetings via phone.

Working from home resulted in my taking on a more passive role. Interestingly, I realized that before, I had far too often unwittingly steered the team in my predetermined direction. Becoming more passive and allowing the associates the opportunity to forge their own path was vital in their growth. We even found ourselves exploring solutions together that otherwise might have been left uncharted.

I discovered some other truths about working from home. Starting a meeting just a minute late is excruciating when you are listening to the silence in your empty home office. Moreover, the three to five minutes wasted as the attendees take their seats and rummage around trying to find paper and pen is intolerable when you are on the other end of a phone line!

As I examined time through a fresh lens, I discovered dysfunction in almost every element of every task completed by the company. Using my newfound knowledge, we were able to introduce some guidelines that created a more efficient and healthier environment. When a leader mandates that the company become masters of time, the team finds that an abundance of time is the reward.

Recognition, Rewards, and Celebration

Great leaders realize that a good dose of recognition and reward is always appreciated. I have found that a reward of money, while it is always welcome, is not a good method of recognizing and rewarding performance. Yes, there should be a bonus program as part of the overall compensation, but I have found that recognition in the form of an experience gives something more valuable to an employee.

If a team member loves golf, an opportunity to play on one of the elite courses in the country might be worth the investment. Even though I do not like golf, I still remember playing Torrey Pines and La Costa more than 30 years ago. On the other hand, I have received dozens of bonuses, but recall little about any of them (except if they failed to meet my expectations.) Other leaders have confirmed to me that this experience is typical.

It's best to know your team members well, so that you can invest in rewards that earn the biggest bang for the buck. Since you are leading a company that has invested in team-building efforts, you probably already have a good grasp on what motivates each member.

Celebrations are another vital part of the interaction between teams and leaders. When you take the time and make the investment to create a singular experience, the memories will last a lifetime. A team dinner at Ruth's Chris steak house is nice… and maybe even memorable. But when three seafood towers and a few bottles of Sassicaia wine are introduced, the event becomes indelible in the minds of the team members. And the expense is peanuts when you consider that the team has just delivered a record year… and is expected to do the same the next year.

Finally, do not forget the value of taking care of the significant others of your employees. Once each year, a team celebration at a destination venue with spouses or significant others will pay meaningful dividends in goodwill. When we show appreciation for those who support the leaders at home, we will receive more buy-in from them. Recognizing and thanking the significant other during the year helps to soften the blow when Mom has to miss a child's concert because of an important meeting with a customer.

Fueling the Fire

When you have assembled a talented team that shares your values, and when the members have divergent personality preferences, you have the ingredients for a winning team. A metamorphosis in team health occurs when we implement a unique blend of working guidelines and team-enhancing habits.

We might institute a policy as simple as: All electronic devices are turned off during meetings. How many times have you poured your soul into a presentation only to feel unappreciated, because others are distracted and fumbling with their phones?

A group of talented people assembled for a common purpose can morph into a vibrant team. Members are talented, involved contributors, each responsible for an essential part of the team's health and success. When working in a culture of organizational cooperation – a healthy environment – the team can transcend into a synergistic unit. Such a team can achieve optimized organizational capacity. Over time, we find ourselves able to complete so much more, with much less effort.

Think of it as a world-class rowing crew, gliding gracefully across the water. Compare that with the image of a ship erratically churning through the turbulence of a stormy sea. Where do you see your team? The ideal of the team of world-class rowers is readily achievable... if the leader has the courage, discipline and desire to make it so. We find that the leaders and other team members become exhilarated as tedious duties transform into enjoyable enlightenments, and the change in approach will spread throughout the enterprise. It is amazingly fulfilling for a leader, and you might even find yourself addicted.

Lighthearted Lesson: A Tale of Two Spouses

At an off-site celebration that included spouses, a young spouse of a relatively new hire drank a bit too much. I offered her a bit of assistance and she vomited, covering the pants I was wearing.

I did not want to embarrass her, so I retired for the evening and her husband helped her to their room. I decided to never mention the matter and thought that only her husband and I had seen what happened. I threw the trousers away; and the matter was never mentioned in my presence after that.

After I retired, I saw her again when I returned to the company for a holiday party. I told her that a decade later, I was still as fond of her as I had been on that first visit.

She looked at me and laughed. "Even though I puked all over you, you still liked me?"

"Indeed," I answered. "You are the only person in my entire career that was so inclined."

On another occasion, I was entertaining an emerging leader and his wife at a hockey game and trying to get them to move to Pittsburgh. As an executive working for a prominent company in the city, I was careful about my alcohol intake in public venues. My guests were not so cautious.

At a break, I went to the concession stand and found that the beer they were drinking was out of stock. I purchased the local brew and returned to the seats, advising them of the change of beverage. One sip in, the woman's face twisted in disgust.

"This beer tastes like ass," she quipped.

A little unsure how to respond, I replied, "I'm not sure what ass tastes like."

"Drink this and you'll know," she answered, shoving the beer in my direction.

The couple ended up joining me in Pittsburgh. I often wondered if the hockey game and my ability to make her feel comfortable played a role in their decision.

CHAPTER 4

Smoke Signals

Listen if you want to be heard.

– **John Wooden**

G reat leaders know that communication is one of the most important – and also one of the most challenging – elements in business to master. If communication is handled improperly, it can break the spirit of the company.

In my first book, *Unbundle It,* I devoted 23 pages to the subject of communication – although the topic permeates the entire work. In this book, we are covering some of the same topics, but I have included some new material from the perspective of a leader.

There is a wide range of communication – from a simple email saying, "Thank you," to a multimedia extravaganza that is broadcast around the globe. In this chapter, we will look at:

A Leader's Role in Communication

A leader sets the tone for the communications program of a company. Excellence in communication requires a blend of discipline, resilience and courage. The most extreme example of discipline in communication that I encountered in my industry was at a company with a zero-profanity policy. A newly-recruited executive happened to curse during a board meeting; the individual was excused from the meeting and terminated afterward. Although that action may seem extreme, I believe that such a level of diligence is required if we want to communicate effectively.

While perfect communication is unachievable, we can definitely get most of it right. Each leader has to determine what the best approach is for his or her company. What is right for one company might not be for another. A leader should consult with stakeholders at all levels in the organization when building a communications program.

The first step is to identify and detail the current state of the company's communications, including the tools currently used. Next, expected outcomes should be decided, and the leader should create the framework for a plan. But drafting the communications plan should be a collaborative process that involves the senior leadership team. One of the biggest challenges facing a leadership team is that they may not even understand what a **good** communication program might look like. Because of that possibility, it might be wise to enlist an outside communications expert.

Once the approach is created and accepted by the leadership team, the leader must insist on compliance from the team. In fact, the leader must insist that all leaders adopt and advocate for the program. Advocacy is a vital element.

Book 1 Leadership: The Responsibility to Ignite

The broader company team will want to understand the answers to two vital questions. The first one is, "How is it going to make my life better?" That question is more commonly heard as, "What's in it for me?" The second question is, "How will each voice be heard?"

Almost every employee wants to be heard. More importantly, they want tangible evidence that leadership has heard them. Even if they receive a hard "no" for an answer, the team member will appreciate that the company listened. And, a hard "no" should include an explanation.

If a leader discovers that a member of his or her leadership team has not bought into the program, or has refused to adopt its principles, that must be addressed. That team member needs to be promptly coached – and if the behavior is not immediately corrected, he or she must be terminated. Moreover, the reason for that termination should be communicated to all. It can be said as simply as: "Joe is no longer with the company. He did not fit the company's values and he will be seeking employment elsewhere. We wish him good luck as he continues his journey elsewhere."

Words Matter

The words that we choose to describe the past, present, or future matter. When describing a situation or philosophy, one company might use the words "blessed," "compete," and "nurture," while another might use "lucky," "fight," and "destroy." The words that are right for one company will not be compatible for another. If you are in the business of manufacturing weapons, the words "fight" and "destroy" might be rather effective.

There are a few words that should not be used in communications, notably "they" and "them." I have learned that "they" and "them" do not really exist, and that using those terms will deflect accountability.

"Can't" is another word to avoid. Usually, "can't" really means "won't," and there is a huge difference in true meaning between the two. I also prefer to outlaw contractions in company communications; contractions have a connotation of laziness.

I have found that it is best to avoid speaking in the negative. Instead of being against something, we should describe what we are in favor of – what we stand for. When we have a differing view from others on a topic, we can simply say, "We wish for a change."

Communication is a Web

Communication is much more than just a two-way street. It is a complex web, shooting out and back in every direction. It is electrified with synapses, firing continuously. When we view communication through that lens, we can better comprehend just how complex it is. Let me share some tools for responding to communications challenges.

There are many best practices to consider in company communications. Town halls, newsletters, meeting protocols, and video messages are some practices that are being used with great success when used purposefully.

There are a few methods that I found especially effective. One is a CAT (Colleagues Around the Table) meeting. And, of course, CAT was an apt acronym for a business focused on companion animal nutrition! Each month, I met with each employee who was having an anniversary; the meeting included a meal.

The meeting would start with a "get-to-know-each-other" conversation, followed by a short update on things happening in the company. Then there would be a question-and-answer period. After almost every meeting, at least one person would hang around and share something that they had been hesitant to mention in the more formal session.

Another method of communication that I favored was the suggestion box. We called our suggestion box Bright Ideas for the President. I had a box installed in each work location, and each Monday, our site-level HR person would open the box and log the ideas. Next, a copy of each submission would be relayed to me. Finally, before the work week ended, I would send each suggester a personal response.

That kind of system requires intense discipline, coupled with a long-term commitment. One must also be prepared to receive nasty comments; they will always be – as one might expect – anonymous. In my company, one of my trusted HR staff members coordinated the program, and one associate at each location helped support the effort.

During the initial phase of a suggestion box program, a leader can expect a bit of chaos. Depending upon the level of team health, there may be a number of unproductive comments. And team health can be different at different sites. At one company I worked for, there were three distinct factories. Within a week, we learned: at one factory, many of the employees were angry; at the second one, the employees were needy; at the third location, employees seemed much more engaged. With suggestion box input, we were able to make some meaningful changes.

Be aware that site leaders generally hate this program; they see it as a snitch box. So, the president or CEO has the responsibility to explain the program to the other company leaders. He or she must explain that, unless a comment should include details of willful misconduct on the part of the site leader, it would be handled in conjunction with site leadership.

In my experience, every comment from the box was discussed with the appropriate site leader, and he or she would have the opportunity to be part of the solution. Written responses to employees often would confirm that the problem was being handled by the site director. In most cases, the site directors ended up loving the program. Issues that they had wanted to see addressed – but had somehow continued – were resolved.

At one of my companies – as a result of this system – an illegal drug ring was identified and quashed. Another location was able to adopt a new, suggested process that became the "gold standard" in the company. We were able to address misunderstandings and avoid long-term ill will.

The suggestion box program is not right for every leader or every company, but if a key leader is committed to it, it can deliver amazing results. One site director at one company seemed overly concerned about the program, to the point of being angry about it. Through the program, we discovered that this particular individual was not aligned with company values; in fact, his conduct bordered on illegal. He was immediately terminated.

Of all the methods I used to connect with team members in remote locations, these were the two most effective. At the same time, they required great effort and discipline from me. Driving four hours to have lunch with eight or nine employees at midnight is not for the faint of heart.

One note of caution: If the top leader and leadership team are not committed to the program, then do not introduce it. As is the case with any new program, poor implementation is worse than not doing it at all.

Walking and Talking

I call one of my favorite methods of enhancing communications **Walking and Talking**. This method might not be effective for every leader, but it became a natural part of my day because of my personality and genuine love for our team members.

I fervently believe that the leader – when possible – should tour the entire company facility (or facilities) and speak to as many employees as he or she can. In my opinion, if you visit a remote site and do not take the time to walk the floor, you are not demonstrating a full commitment to your company.

When you take that initiative, it speaks more loudly to show your desire to communicate than any town hall, video update, or other more easily-implemented tool. Make no mistake – all of those tools are very effective, but if you truly want your team to know that you care, Walking and Talking will pay huge dividends. As a bonus, others in senior leadership will start doing the same, and the overall results will amaze everyone. Employee engagement will rise, well-being will soar, and almost every KPI (key performance indicator) will improve.

These walks are not formal group tours. And they should not be overtly critical. But a leader can discover a great number of issues (and potential issues) as he or she walks through the work area. You simply stop by each workstation, greet the team members, and ask a few questions. It's amazing what you will learn.

At one of my companies, we had an amazing leadership team on site. They were fair, kind, and genuine with all employees. Despite all their efforts, almost every time I walked the floor I learned about a small issue that – if left uncorrected – could have become more serious. One time, it was a tiny water leak that created an unsafe condition; another time, there was a need for a small step-stool that would have made a shorter team member's job easier.

This company had made the decision to play streamed music throughout the facility. It was a huge hit; the employees loved the gesture. The result was improved output in every department. It even became a retention tool, as team members loved working for the company because of the music. It was not something that was done at other similar companies.

One day, I entered the plant and began Walking and Talking. A packaging line had been relocated a few days earlier. As I engaged the team working there, one member asked me if the speaker for the sound system could be moved so that they could better enjoy the music. Obviously, not relocating the speaker was an oversight on the part of management, and it could easily be remedied.

After my walk, I entered the site leader's office and asked him about the speaker. He agreed to have the speaker moved and directed a maintenance team member to do it. He seemed a bit disappointed, though; he told me that he had visited that team at least three times since it had been moved. He could not understand why no one there had ever mentioned the speaker concern to him or any of the line leads.

It was a small issue and this particular leader was a great person, but he had not connected with his team in a way so they would feel comfortable raising such a concern with him. He saw that Walking and Talking worked, and that day, a new 'walker and talker' was born.

Many will suggest that, for larger companies, this type of tool is not possible. It is true that as a company scales in size, it is nearly impossible for one leader to walk every site. However, if every leader on the leadership team walks one site, the results will still amaze. Sam Walton, the founder of Walmart, was known to walk through the stores, the warehouses, and other facilities on a regular basis. The results are part of business history.

Employee Surveys

Employee surveys have been around longer than I have. Most, however, are the epitome of form over substance. The team goes through the paces of filling out the paperwork, and little is learned. Worse, almost nothing ever changes.

Surveys that are properly executed and analyzed can become some of the most important tools available to a leader. Information in surveys can result in meaningful change that enhances company performance. Nevertheless, surveys are a long-term commitment; analyzing changes over the years will reveal if the organization is becoming healthier (or not).

When creating a survey, keep a few things in mind. The structure of the questions can influence a person's response, so make certain that questions are written carefully. Questions should be asked in a way that we can easily discover key drivers of satisfaction or dissatisfaction. We want to ask questions that examine each aspect of the company.

It is also important that the number of employees is large enough so they can believe the survey is anonymous. If employees realize that the survey is only being given to a few people, you will probably not get honest responses. Employees are smarter than we often give them credit for; most care deeply, and they want the things they like to continue and those they do not care for to end.

Consider hiring a consulting group that specializes in surveys to run the program. Such contracts are rather inexpensive, and the quality of results is far more important than the small cost of the program.

After the surveys are analyzed, it is important that action be taken in a visible and timely fashion. When the employees realize that the leadership genuinely cares about their well-being, performance will improve. And then, the second survey will be far more effective than the first, because employees will be more transparent.

Through surveys, we can learn much about problems that need to be fixed. At one company, we learned that the team health was very high – except in two select segments. In the third shift in the packaging department, a poor leader had been mistreating employees. It was amazing – for nearly eight months, the situation had gone on, and no one at the top leadership level had suspected any issue. It was revealing that the other departments on the same shift scored meaningfully higher than that packaging team.

The other group that was troubled was the main office. Those closest to leadership were disgruntled – how could that be? We discovered a misunderstanding, and that a rumor that had not been properly quashed was the source. The problem was easily resolved.

At another company, middle management scored far lower than their superiors – and lower than those they led. It was an astounding, yet disquieting result. It turned out that the leader at a new remote office site had allowed that location's team to enjoy a company-funded, expensive gourmet coffee service. Meanwhile, the managers at headquarters were relegated to regular coffee. That practice led to rumors that one team did not have to work as many hours, which created resentment. More than a decade later, I am amazed that none of the top leadership ever heard a whisper about the situation until we did the survey. It was so ridiculous that I coined the term Coffeegate to describe it. It was an example of a failure in leadership – but one that we were able to correct, because of a survey.

Team Health Assessments

A great tool to quickly evaluate weaknesses in a team are team health assessments. During my time in consulting, I performed dozens of

Book 1 Leadership: The Responsibility to Ignite

these analyses, and they always delivered outstanding results. Unlike employee surveys, team assessments are not undertaken anonymously. They are also only completed by a very select group, usually with 15 to 20 senior leaders. Results, however, are kept anonymous when shared in detail with the larger team.

Each area of focus is scored; strengths and weaknesses can be discussed, and corrective action – if required – can be taken. Usually, the assessment reveals that trust is a major issue. If that is the case, it must be addressed. Without trust, the team will never meet its potential.

With one client, I discovered an assessment misalignment that was statistically significant. Normally, a close-knit team will answer questions showing a general alignment. On a 1 to 5 scale, most team members will score 1 to 3 on items where there is dissatisfaction. Similarly, areas of strength typically score from 3 to 5. Such ranges are expected, because there are always some team members who are harsher scorers, and others who are more lenient. Almost never do we see a 2 score and a 5 score as a response to the same question.

With the assessment in question, two team members answered over half of the questions in a drastically different way from the remaining members of the team. It was concerning, and I shared the results with the senior executive. We decided to do some interviews and some 360 assessments on the two people. 360 assessments are, as the term might suggest, based on anonymous input from key employees that have an association with the individual being assessed.

Superiors, peers, subordinates, and even people who were not necessarily direct reports were asked to rate the two individuals. As I expected, the assessments revealed very troubling behaviors. I recommended that both members of the team be terminated for cause. They were, and there was an immediate improvement of team health that day.

Emails

Email is a technology that has revolutionized communication. It is a very powerful tool, and it can make communication much more effective. But almost every communication tool has a downside, and emails have plenty of downsides. Emails have been overused to the point that many people have hundreds – or even thousands – that are left unopened and unread. Also, individuals tend to hide behind emails. Texts are similar to emails – easy to use, helpful with productivity – but they can lead to laziness in communication.

The biggest problem with anything written is that the impact of immediate communication is lost. There are three elements that create the entirety of communication. The first element is the actual words. However, communication experts agree that words account for only 7 percent of the total communication. So, when we write to someone, we lose 93 percent of the communication's potential impact. The recipient may not understand the intended tone of the communication. For example, if an email is sent to an employee involving a potentially volatile issue, the employee may read it with the harshest tone imaginable, completely misunderstanding the intent.

Tone and tenor account for 43 percent of communication impact. When we choose to communicate over the phone, we significantly enhance the overall impact of our message.

So, words and tone account for 50 percent of communication; body language makes up the other half. Being in the same room with someone allows for a better exchange of information. The revolution of video conferencing has allowed visual interaction that is almost as good as an in-person meeting.

Book 1 Leadership: The Responsibility to Ignite

In *Unbundle It*, I created a detailed list of email dos and don'ts. I now include it here, because 10 years later I believe it is still relevant (and almost no one adopts them all):

1. **Never send an email when you are angry.** I advocate a cooling-off period before addressing any dicey topics. Email is never the appropriate format to discuss a sensitive subject. As we learned earlier, the text alone accounts for less than 10 percent of communication; if you are angry and the issue is sensitive, even 10 percent isn't going to cut it. Take the direct, face-to-face approach after cooling off. It always works best.

2. **Never address a sensitive or emotionally-charged topic via email.** In addition to creating significant organizational strife, the tone, tenor, and body language that the recipients add when reading the email to their friends is usually exaggerated.

3. **Eliminate the use of return receipts.** They have no place in the business world. Does anyone send them back?

4. **Mandate that "Reply to all" emails are not allowed.** It is far too easy to hit "Reply to all" and clog the email server with unimportant gibberish. If it is important enough to send, your employees should type in each recipient's name; the auto-fill feature makes it an easy task. Cultures that allow "Reply to all" emails create drag in the organization. Inevitably, someone will get so used to doing it that an embarrassing mistake will occur.

   Once, an employee and his wife filled in their paperwork for the company's new health-care system. Out of habit, he replied to all with his email response.

   It was a company-wide message. We all had fun with it.

5. **Eliminate one-word emails.** I am perplexed as to why they are ever sent, but I get them regularly.

6. **Be cognizant of string or multiple-message emails.** End users may be able to go back into the email history and find sensitive or inflammatory information.

   Once, my organization was in a dispute with a less-than-ethical customer, and we received a flowery email from them explaining their situation. At the end of the message, they mentioned what an important partnership we had. But a simple scroll down through the email chain revealed the directive from one of their executives: "Tell them what you need to, so they will ship the order. We just won't pay them."

7. **Ensure that emails requiring a response are addressed promptly.** Often, receivers of emails forget to respond to requests in a timely fashion. I have heard a myriad of excuses. The fact is, the failure to acknowledge an email creates problems. It can leave the sender wondering if the email was received; it can result in needed information not being received in time; or, it can leave the sender feeling that you do not respect them enough to respond. Not responding to an email erodes trust and creates drag; therefore, it is vital that messages get timely attention. One of three types of response is acceptable:
   - Answer the question or provide information
   - Request clarification
   - Acknowledge the message and advise when you will reply

8. **Do not expect answers from CC recipients.** It sounds obvious, but I have been amazed by the number of times individuals have asked me if I received their email and why I didn't respond. When I advise that I rarely respond to CC emails, they seem surprised.

Social Media Policies

If your company does not have a social media policy, you need one and you need it immediately. There is no upside to being lenient with employees on social media use at work or if it involves anything work-related. Exceptions might be approved if you happen to be an influencer or if you work at a company where social media is mission-critical.

I believe that the company should establish a zero-tolerance policy. No unauthorized use of social media that pertains to any aspect of a team member's employment should be permitted. That would include work-related posting or commenting at home or posting or commenting during work hours. You can mandate this; you can make it a requirement. The policy should be in writing, and should be signed and acknowledged by each team member. Unless the use of social media is purposeful and specifically authorized, there is no upside to employees using it for any company purpose. There are a mountain of examples that illustrate the reasons for having such a policy.

One employee at my company – a very talented person – was proud of a team accomplishment. He posted a picture on social media, crowing about the capability of his team. On the surface, that kind of publicity seems great. But we had a policy that did not permit any pictures to be taken in the plant.

So, posting the picture violated a crucial policy. And in fact, the picture showed some of a customer's products in the background. We had a contract with the customer that explicitly prohibited us from revealing its products, as one of the products in the photo had not yet launched. Someone from the customer's company saw the picture, and predictably, the response was unpleasant.

Another time, someone posted a picture and some commentary of our softball team playing in a tournament. We had been assigned to play against the Special Olympics team. It was a part of a well-known community effort to help enhance the well-being of the Olympians. I was never more proud of our team; each member allowed the Olympians to make contributions during the contest. It was, by all accounts, a wonderful game. My wife and I watched every minute and stayed afterward; the teams embraced before leaving the field.

But the picture and commentary were misconstrued by one member of the community. She blasted us on social media. The post went viral, and we became known as a cruel company that mocked special-needs people. I received no less than a dozen letters. To describe them as disparaging would be an understatement.

We were able to finally recover after weeks of image repairing and a large donation, coupled with a promise to volunteer at future Special Olympics events. Fallout from the incident remained for over a year. Some continued to refer to us as the company that mocked the disadvantaged.

I recommend that the company have a purposeful social media review team. And anyone on the team should be properly vetted before they are hired.

For example, in my company, we hired a woman to work on our sales team, who frankly would never have been allowed to join the team if we had properly looked into her social media. There were rumors that she had a promiscuous social media presence. However, both the manager and the woman we hired said that anything she had done on social media was in the past.

I believed both people were lying. Since we did not have a formal social media program or policy, I decided to personally investigate.

Both culprits blocked me from any viewing, but I created a fake account.

My fake persona was immediately accepted by her. Her first communication with me was to ask me to find six other friends to join, and then she would send me seminude pictures.

There are another dozen outrageous examples of social media abuse rolling around in my head, but you get the point. Both well-intentioned and spurious activity will create issues for the team if you fail to put a good social media policy in place.

Difficult Conversations

Difficult conversations in the workplace are commonplace. If you are not engaging in conversations with members of your team to correct behaviors, then you are failing them. Even our best employees have blind spots, which can be disruptive.

How we handle these conversations is the difference between a learning experience and a debilitating distraction. In a difficult conversation, people often raise their voice to be heard. There are many conversational styles that can facilitate difficult conversations; there are four styles that I use quite successfully.

The first is to adopt a **standard of discovery** versus a standard of perfection. Perfection draws a line that is rigid. "Right or wrong" or "black or white" describe the perfection standard. When we insist on a perfection standard, we create a culture of winners and losers.

But when we focus on discovery, we probe for information. In the end, we will probably end up in the same place. With discovery, we have **winners** and **learners**. If someone else must lose for us to win, we crush the other's self-esteem. Transitioning to an educational standard lifts the team member's self-worth and promotes further introspection. The fear of criticism or failure is defused.

Advocacy and inquiry is another very good approach. One party clearly states their position and explains, without allowing emotion to creep in, why they are for that position. The second party then has the opportunity to ask questions. Both parties must be trained to ensure that the process is followed properly. When a party is permitted to ask questions and is allowed to voice their view, they are far more likely to accept a position that differs from theirs.

Active listening is an excellent tool when the topic is potentially volatile. In active listening, the guidelines require that the receiving party repeat back what they heard. Once that position is confirmed, the receiving party can state, "So we are agreed on that point" or "Now I understand your position."

If disagreement remains, more questions can probe into how the situation can be improved. Questions such as, "What would make it better?" can facilitate the conversation. A pivot is an effective tactic when using active listening: "If we cannot follow your preferred path, what would be the next best approach?"

Active listening introduces empathy, and since you're a great leader, you have plenty of that to go around. Active listening takes time and extra effort; but when the matter is resolved, the well-being and relational capital is very robust.

One of my favorite tactics is to persuade the other party to come up with the solution that you advocate instead of giving the solution to them. Explain the problem and ask their opinion on how to resolve it. You can ask, "Have you thought of this as a possible solution?" while weaving your idea into the conversation. That conversation can continue until there is a final resolution.

I have discovered there are a couple of outcomes from this approach. First, you get buy-in from the employee, and once they feel that they have ownership, the solution is easily implemented. Second, and more importantly, they may find a flaw in your approach. The resulting solution will probably turn out to be far better than the original one that you had proposed. The result: you have an engaged, motivated team member.

Cultural Differences

Some differences can be seen – people come in multiple shapes, sizes, and skin colors – and some cannot. To be an effective leader and to work well with a team, we must be aware of all the differences that have the potential to create issues. Sometimes, people can look almost identical, but there may be vast unseen cultural differences.

A great example comes from our neighbor to the north. Canadians tend to see Americans as rude and almost heartless. We can easily insult them just by being ourselves.

In Brazil, the "OK" hand gesture is the equivalent to raising your middle finger. In our culture, a bride wears white, and black is associated with death. In many Asian cultures, brides wear red – and white is associated with death.

If we want to build trust and enhance communication, we must learn to be aware of cultural differences – both seen and unseen. Think of someone's cultural background as a tree. For all of the branches and leaves that you see, there is an equally large root system that is never exposed. We must discover those cultural roots and prepare ourselves to modify our style, so that we can optimize our communication. There are plenty of cultural elements to be addressed. Educate yourself on them and become an expert.

Pulling It All Together

There is a significant amount to learn on the topic of communication; we have only scratched the surface here. I hope you will take away two universal principles that I believe comprise the gold standard in communication. First, always be honest. Second, bad news will usually travel faster than good news. So, those who have the courage to report bad news in an honest and timely manner should be rewarded. Admitting when a situation is not good will build trust, and will lead to more productive communications.

Above all, keep communication lines open throughout your organization. When it comes to business, the term "the silence is deafening" is more appropriately modified to "the silence is debilitating."

Lighthearted Lessons: Out of Touch and Inappropriate

Being out of touch as a leader can lead to negative results. Early in my career, I had a job where the executive leadership did not invest anything in relationships with team members – at any level. But at the same time, the CEO decided that he wanted to connect with the team, and so he recorded a video. In the video he referred to the employees as a family. The reaction was swift and far-reaching. One of the managers commented to me, "That confirms it. He is into incest. What he's been doing to us for years… and we are his family." (That quote was sanitized for publication.) The company eventually had to file for bankruptcy.

At a later point in my career, while we were grappling with our social media policy, we had a manager who was of suspect moral character. He seemed addicted to hiring women for their looks over their character. To be blunt, he was not looking for church girls.

Book 1 Leadership: The Responsibility to Ignite

One woman he hired would charge more than $1,000 of personal expenses on her corporate credit card, later claiming they were business expenses. She also committed to an unauthorized $20,000 advertising program. And, the ad buy came with two club-level season tickets to her alma mater's football program (a fact she conveniently forgot to mention at first).

I worked with the university to undo the commitment, and her employment was terminated. Immediately, she filed suit for wrongful discharge, and made an accusation of sexual harassment. In her lawsuit, she claimed that her manager had regularly harassed her on social media. I was no fan of that creep – the manager – but since he was a friend of the owner, I had to keep him on the team.

I met with him and asked him if there was any truth to her assertions. I recall telling him that if there was anything, I needed to know immediately. He started sobbing, and promised me that there was nothing. He even claimed to be insulted by her accusations.

Our response to the lawsuit included the results of our investigation; we confirmed that we had found no credibility to her claims. Her attorney then responded with a ream of paper with screenshots from Facebook exchanges. In one instance, she had posted a picture of herself in a bikini holding a fish. The manager who had hired her had commented on the post, saying that the bikini "must have made her boyfriend's worm hard, because his worm was hard just looking at the picture." Disgusting.

I was incredulous. The manager's comments were not only harassing, they were revolting. I confronted the manager with the evidence, but he simply manufactured more tears and claimed he had forgotten.

CHAPTER 5

Spreading Like Wildfire – Your Wildfire

Brand is just a perception, and
perception will match reality over time.

– Elon Musk

Every company is unique, each with its own image. One of the vital investments that leads to success is branding. The most important brand of all, the company itself, is often overlooked. I assure you that if you are not investing in your company's image, you are failing to tap into a significant opportunity. Successful branding can propel a company forward at warp speed.

Branding is both an internally- and externally-focused effort. The result of a good branding program is team member loyalty that spreads like a wildfire through the company, the community, the industry – and possibly even around the globe.

The notion of branding has been hard-coded in me since childhood. At age 8 or 9, my father and I drove past an automotive plant. My father commented that the company employee parking lot was filled with cars that had been made by other manufacturers. He said, "This factory will fail unless the leadership instills in the employees a better loyalty to their product. If they are not proud enough of the product they make to buy it themselves, then how can they expect anyone else to buy it?" A year later, the plant was closed.

Fast-forward 30 years. I went to work for a company that was known for making great catsup. I didn't work in the catsup division; and more importantly, I do not like catsup. But, for 11 long years, I used my company's catsup every time I came upon it in a restaurant. As an executive at the company, I saw it as vital that I visibly demonstrate my loyalty to the company – regardless of my personal preference.

Great leaders know how to build loyalty and a following. Some leaders are so successful at branding that their brand catches fire and becomes synonymous with the product category. Some companies have been investing in brand awareness for generations.

Take, for example, Coca-Cola. When I was a child, Coke was "teaching the world to sing," to paraphrase a popular commercial. In an ad, a football player – arguably the most dangerous in the league – transforms into the epitome of kindness after having a Coke. The player was so mean that his nickname was Mean Joe Greene. The message was clear: Coca-Cola was synonymous with happiness and making the world a better place. It is rather amazing – 50 years later, the message, while it has evolved, is still about Coke making things better. Coke is so much a part of our lives that many in certain regions of the United States use the name as a ubiquitous term for a dark-colored, cold, carbonated, sugar-based drink.

There are many examples where a brand has become synonymous with the product: Kleenex, Band-Aid, Weed Eater, Jacuzzi, and Q-Tips

Book 1 Leadership: The Responsibility to Ignite

are but a few of the brands that have morphed into our everyday lexicon to stand for an entire category.

Branding in sports teams is a remarkable phenomenon. So intense is the loyalty of a team's fan base that billions of dollars are spent by fans as they seek to be part of the magic. Fans buy jerseys, have their bodies tattooed, and paint their cars to demonstrate their commitment to a sports team. Every year, hundreds – if not thousands – of fights break out over team loyalty. Fans have become so crazed that riots have broken out in cities after wins and losses. Celebratory parades line the streets in the cities of the champions. "My team won," is the proud refrain.

"My team?" Is the fan a part-owner? Does he or she make money from being affiliated with the team? The answer to these questions is almost always no. In fact, the contrary is likely to be true. Fans invest money in tickets, events, and merchandise – they fund the owners' and players' lavish lifestyles. In many ways, the team owns them.

I was a rabid sports fan for most of my life. It became almost an obsession. When my team lost, I found myself in a bad mood. I spent tens of thousands of dollars following my team. My home was described as a shrine to sports. I want to report that I'm better now, and while I still enjoy watching sports, the extreme fervor has left me.

But why do these brands and teams become so ingrained into a fan's psyche? It's all about marketing and building the brand. A strong brand creates intense loyalty, lighting a fire within the consumer. And it takes great leaders to build brand loyalty and a following.

I find it amazing that many leaders fail to make the investment in a vital brand – their business name. If we examine branding while considering the purpose of the business, cultivating awareness of – and loyalty to – that business might be the most important goal of all.

Can you imagine the employees of a company tattooing their company logo on their body? Can you imagine a celebration turning into a riot after record-setting bonuses were paid to every team member?

However, where we work is a choice, and I would acknowledge that most people work at a company out of convenience or need. We've all heard the reasoning: "I need to feed my family and the factory is close to where I live, so I work there." "The company has a schedule that complements mine." "It pays the bills."

But imagine if each employee loved their employer. Yes, they would still need the money, but their zeal for their work would drive them to transform into advocates for the enterprise. They would simply not contemplate working elsewhere. It is a situation worth visualizing.

They Once Burned Brightly, but No More

Some of the greatest companies of our time have made such an investment to create a memorable brand. Others seem to have lost their way. Southwest Airlines is one such company. A decade or more ago, they were a topic of conversation due to their unique approach. Their employees were their biggest advocates, followed closely by their customers. Although their lower fares were an enticement, customers found that the Southwest experience, from ticket purchase to baggage claim, was refreshing.

I recall attending a class on customer service. The instructor passed around examples of letters written by customers to companies, along with the replies that the companies sent. One letter was from a Southwest customer who was angry over the fact that flight attendants had been joking during the preflight briefing. The letter ended, "I will

Book 1 Leadership: The Responsibility to Ignite

never fly your airline again." The purported response from Southwest was short and included the sentence, "We will miss you."

Fast-forward to today. Southwest is in the news, but for all the wrong reasons. Employees are regularly complaining about the company. Consumers are livid over the poor service. What happened? I believe that leadership must take responsibility for Southwest's fall from its lofty position. *Wait a minute,* you might think, *Southwest remains on the list of best companies.* That is still technically true, but it's a lagging indicator. Unless leadership rights the ship promptly, that status will disappear.

Another example of a company that has seen a similar decline is Walmart. In the 1970s and '80s, Walmart was a phenomenon. Communities would cheer when a Walmart came to their town. To consumers, Walmart did not just represent a shopping errand – it was a destination. Much like Southwest, it offered an economical yet enjoyable experience. And it was known as a desirable place to work.

Shortly after the turn of the millennium, I had the opportunity to fly on a private plane with the president of Kroger. It was just the two of us, and we had a most interesting conversation. He shared his frustration over the lack of loyalty from his employees. He knew that Kroger paid their associates nearly double what Walmart did – and Kroger's benefits were far better, too – but there was no loyalty. He was a brilliant man, yet he was completely stymied by the apparent incongruity. Because I had partnered with Walmart for nearly 20 years, I was able to give him a perspective.

"It's like a cult," I offered. I explained that the enigma that was Walmart started with intense training and nurturing of employees. At that time, every employee was a shareholder, and the stock price was listed in every facility, usually near the break room. The sign reminded employees that where the stock closed on the next day was up to them.

The company engaged in employee rallies where songs were sung as part of the sessions. Those famous Saturday-morning meetings were akin to Southern Baptist revivals. I was fortunate enough to be asked to attend one such meeting; I was even allowed to take the stage and participate in the Walmart dance! (Yes, there is a Walmart dance.)

As the Walmart experience applied to consumers, many felt fortunate to be able to shop there. Some drove well over an hour to have the opportunity to walk the aisles. Low prices were a great incentive, but there was so much more. A friendly person warmly greeted every customer, and each child received a smiley-face that became a Walmart symbol of pride and belonging. Those smiley-faces became ubiquitous and immediately recognizable as part of the Walmart brand; they stood for excitement, low prices, and a pleasant experience. Associates were both welcoming and knowledgeable.

What is your image of Walmart today? Most people I ask about Walmart shop there out of necessity. Long lines, crowded and cluttered stores, and relatively unhelpful associates translate into a less than enjoyable experience these days. But people still flock to Walmart out of need. The prices are still low, and so the shoppers still find their way there. Still, many consumers change to other options as soon as their economic situations allow it.

Once again, the decline must be placed on the shoulders of the leadership. Poor leaders hate to admit that they have failed. They look for excuses. In this case, many will argue that COVID-19 and the rise of the online marketplace have had a negative impact – and that is true, in part. Nevertheless, making those excuses is simplistic and lazy. Giving those reasons for decline might soothe the leadership team's egos, but if Walmart was truly the destination it once was, consumers would eagerly look forward to their shopping trip there. Walmart – it was once great, and it remains good. But that simply is not good enough.

Personal Fires Waiting to be Lit

So how do we do it? How do we become that perceived pinnacle of excellence? The answer is simple: successful branding, fostered by leadership.

During the first half of my career, I was employed at two large consumer products companies. Both boasted mega-brands, and those brands were household names across the country. I suppose that both companies were considered good places to work, but neither invested much time, money, or effort in building the team. We had plenty of programs that were aimed at building teamwork, yet there was no buy-in from the top. The employees all knew that the programs were merely superficial displays. The "fad du jour," many would call each of the programs.

Nevertheless, I loved working for both companies, and I spent nine years with one and 11 with the other. The second was far better than the first, but it still lacked the personal touch of a Walmart in that era.

I became an executive at the second company, and in the boardroom I felt truly out of place. I was successful, and my teams delivered good quarterly numbers and never missed, but it just was not an environment where I thrived. As I said earlier in this book, it was not the leaders themselves that were the issue, it was the culture at the company that molded the leaders into the people they had become.

The company was the epitome of a siloed structure, with three divisions in North America. Each division was a billion-dollar entity, yet there was almost zero interface between the teams. The first six years of my time there, I did not know a single person who worked for either of the other two divisions. There was no sharing of news of wins or losses. There was no continuity. Looking back on my tenure, I realize what a significant lost opportunity it was.

The image of our division in the marketplace was, at best, neutral. One of my responsibilities was overseeing customer service. The team was exceptional; they delivered best-in-class service to our customers. Our logistics people were reliable, too, and equally outstanding.

We were regularly pummeled by the sales team, though; our customers seemed never to be happy with our performance. Regularly, we were reminded that one of our largest competitors was superior. It was suggested that maybe we could take a page out of their playbook.

Fortuitously, we ended up buying that competitor. I then found myself overseeing customer service and logistics for the entire new entity. I was excited. I wanted to learn the former competitor's ways and to see what "great" truly looked like.

Amazingly, they were worse on every index than we were. Their orders were late, products were out of stock, and damage levels were all chronically inferior to the levels we had enjoyed. So why the disparity? How was it that internal and external stakeholders all agreed they were exceptional?

The answer was: branding. Branding had been fostered through leadership's buy-in. It amounted to an intentional outreach to all stakeholders that trumpeted that their service team was cutting-edge and led the industry. They literally wrote a book on excellence in service. They attended every industry think-tank and had polished speakers who were adept at self-promotion.

Book 1 Leadership: The Responsibility to Ignite

Their practices provided a great lesson for me, and I realized that image appeared to be far more important than actual results.

When I joined my next company, I found a far healthier culture. The new company had its own set of issues, but internal and external stakeholders agreed that the company was exceptional. It was a family-owned business, and they truly embodied the term "family" throughout the organization.

My first sales call there was with a leader of a very large customer – one who I had just visited when I was with my previous employer. My earlier meeting with him had gone very poorly; I was tense, and hoped that he had forgotten me.

When he entered the room, he smiled broadly, and said "Elliott Haverlack, it is great to see you." He added, "Sorry about the ass-kicking I gave you last month."

He proceeded to tell me that he literally hated doing business with my previous employer and enjoyed abusing its team members. He referred to my former company as its own worst enemy. He also told me that he felt that his negative treatment of the company's associates bought him leverage.

Well, I can assure you that, as dysfunctional as the tactic was, the leverage worked. We had been terrified of him, and the result was that his company received significantly more attention than other comparable companies.

My new company had a great image in the community. I learned that a decade before my arrival, leadership had shut down the factory for a weekend and had taken the entire team – including spouses – to the Bahamas. One day, after I had been at that organization for about 10 years, I found myself having lunch at a bar about 50 miles away from work. The bartender and I struck up a conversation. When I mentioned who I worked for, she became almost giddy. She chattered, "That's a great company; they take their employees to the Bahamas."

By that time, 20 years had passed since that Bahamas trip, but the image of the company's goodness continued to permeate throughout the community. The fire that was lit 20 years earlier was still burning brightly. The cost of that trip proved to be inconsequential in comparison to the goodwill it created.

Spreading the Fire

Creating an image that transcends what the public perceives as normal requires a desire to become exceptional. As an organization, we need to ask the question, "Is this an exceptional business?" and then answer it with a resounding "Yes!" Leadership must be able to describe what makes the company extraordinary. And, they should be able to do that with the same level of passion as when they talk about the company's vision. Creating a mission, vision, and values that can easily be socialized – both internally and externally – must happen before the branding effort can commence.

Every building, every desk, and every lunchroom should include visible reminders of who and what the company is, and where the company is going. Each meeting should start with a reference to the company's initiative. Leaders need to drive that message and embed it into the skin of the enterprise.

Our employees, as our most valuable asset, should be enlisted to trumpet the great news throughout the organization. As I mentioned earlier, we can enlist employees to become brand ambassadors, with the hope that they will evolve into brand evangelists.

This kind of initiative needs a name, and I have used the name Culture Warrior Program with much success. Such a program will

Book 1 Leadership: The Responsibility to Ignite

live or die on the shoulders of the leader. But when it's carried out properly, it's effective.

At one of my companies, when a prospective customer was visiting, we had shirts made up with the customer logo. As we walked through the factory, it was an awe-inspiring sight for the customer reps to see 100 smiling associates, all wearing shirts emblazoned with their logo. It was a dramatic demonstration of how important the customer was to us. Shirts, hats, backpacks – all carrying the same message – become part of an image that communicates what is in the company's soul. Soon, the message starts to make its way out to the broader community, and the public starts to think about that company in a whole new favorable light.

At one company, we handed out T-shirts to all team members. A few weeks later, I was in a store in a town a half-hour away with my "Culture Warrior" shirt on, and I encountered a fellow employee who I had not yet met. She, too, was wearing her shirt. We had a nice chat, and I was pleased to see that the program was working.

Leaders who convince themselves that galvanizing employees is an impossible task and believe that people will not get that excited about something so simplistic are the worst kind of leaders. They have become so disconnected with the team that they fail to realize that the vast majority of their employees desperately want something to rally around.

Rallying cries become a vital part of the program. "Better Together" and "Every Day You Get Our Best" are two slogans I have used in the past. While volunteering for a children's charity, we used "Better Starts Here." What a powerful message!

I always use the example of a political campaign to show how easy it can be. They are mostly volunteers, but campaign workers go crazy for their candidate. They go above and beyond – and to what end?

Victory, of course. That same kind of fervor is in many of your team members at work; we just need to unlock it, and put it on steroids.

Indeed, this intentional type of branding takes a significant investment, but it is worth every second of time and dollar spent. It is a long-term commitment and it should constantly be refreshed and nurtured.

But we see the intangible benefits when the successful brand starts to bleed into the external world. The company becomes the talk of the town... or the country, in larger enterprises. Recruitment of the best talent becomes much easier. Prospective trading partners will break your door down to do business with you. Why? Because people want to be associated with a winner.

External Burning

There are three major external stakeholders to be considered in branding. They include customers, consumers, and the public at large. We might even want to include a fourth – the competitors. In some businesses, the customers are also the consumers. However, in the field that I worked most of my career in, the consumer was the end user and the customers were the retailers who sold the products to consumers.

Here is a story of how branding can change things. My wife and I owned a mid-sized business in the town where she grew up. By most accounts, we were a good place to work, but a misguided sense of humility kept us from trumpeting that fact. Internally, we had buy-in from the employees, and they were truly our biggest asset. We rewarded them with celebrations on a regular basis. My wife took on the role of a nurturing mother to her 350 'children' who called the company home. She regularly loaned team members money and worked tirelessly to ensure all were treated with dignity and respect.

Book 1 Leadership: The Responsibility to Ignite

We hired a new leader; he wanted to start to market our – as he called it – 'rare and exceptional' culture. We commissioned a billboard to be put up along the largest highway entering town. 'Excellence' was the operative word. The billboard was a highly-visible landmark, announcing that we were, indeed, 'excellent.' Our new leader carefully implemented a marketing campaign, and within a year, we were on the list of fastest-growing companies in America. In the second year of the campaign, our company was named the best place to work in our city.

I challenged the leader to land us a spot on the cover of an industry publication. Finally, on the day we sold the business, he presented me with the latest edition of a leading industry periodical. There he was on the cover, smiling broadly with his two canine companions.

What had changed? The answer was clear: branding.

Simply stated, it is not good enough to be a great place to work. Exceptional people and exceptional companies need to be in the news. Intentional branding is a game-changer.

Lighthearted Lesson: Brand-building... or Not

Humor is an important part of life, especially when there are changes to go through. That large consumer product goods company – the one I mentioned earlier, with the siloed structure – decided to tear down the silos. Employees from three disparate divisions were forced into one homogenous entity.

It was a turbulent time. One of my new employees was a brilliant young man with multiple degrees. At one point, he informed me that he had a dog who was an important part of his family.

"What do you feed her?" I asked.

He revealed that her diet was made by one of our competitors. But the competitive product had no special formulation.

"Are you aware that the company who employs you makes diets that are equal to, or better than, the one you are feeding your dog?" I asked.

He replied that his wife bought the dog food. So, I wrote his wife a heartfelt letter, urging her to switch diets; she complied. I sometimes wonder what she thought when she received a personal letter from a company vice president, asking her about her dog's diet.

Shortly afterward, I resigned from that company, and announced that I was going to lead the competitor. At that time, my former employee's wife drafted me a nice letter, asking me if it was OK to change back to the dog's previous formula. I assured her that I was fine with that decision – but I advised that she should check with her husband, since he still worked for company A.

The company that I joined had a unique culture. It had been family-owned and operated for 68 years. There was a legend in the company that one day the owner had walked through the factory handing out $100 bills.

I was hired to move the company to a professionally-managed model. To say that I was a fish out of water was an understatement.

Shortly after my arrival, it was National Safety Week. I proudly hopped into the lunchroom and addressed the team members who were enjoying their lunch. I pulled a twenty out of my wallet and announced that I would give $20 to anyone who could answer a safety question.

The response was silence.

After an uncomfortable pause, an old man looked up from his soup bowl and uttered, "Boy, we don't answer questions around here for less than $100."

Defeated, I returned the twenty to my wallet and slunk out of the room. Even a decade later, I never tried that stunt again there. But it had worked at every other previous factory where I had tried it. In fact, $5 or $10 normally elicited thunderous responses.

CHAPTER 6

When the Fire is Doused

The ultimate measure of a man is not where he stands in the moments of comfort, but where he stands at times of challenge and controversy.

– Reverend Martin Luther King Jr.

I f you are leading a vibrant, cutting-edge organization, chances are that you are in the middle of – or just coming out of – a crisis. Or possibly, you are heading into one and don't know it yet! Frankly, crises are part of the journey. Certainly, it is best to plan so that unnecessary crises are avoided, but to think you can plan your way out of all crises is a fool's errand.

At the same time, good leaders train their team on how to conduct itself during a crisis. Since we cannot avoid crises, we need to learn to become extremely competent at handling them. In fact, the saying, "Use your peace time wisely," was never more true than in dealing with crisis management.

I was once asked what I thought would be the biggest challenge that my company would face in the future. My answer? "Something we don't know about today." My belief is, if you know what is coming, you will have no problem dealing with it. It is the unknown that creates havoc and catapults the organization into crisis.

Crises can take many shapes and forms. They can come in many forms: a random or unexpected event, a public relations blunder, a customer relations conflict, or a human resources issue. While each crisis has its own unique components, they all have a couple of things in common. First, they suck energy and time out of the organization; and second, they all come with some level of pain.

A Failure to Plan... is a Plan to Fail

Appropriate planning is the most important part of having a good crisis management program. In dealing with crises, time is a huge consideration. Even an hour or two can make a significant difference.

Proper planning includes the creation of a core crisis leadership team. The plan should include the names and contact information for all members of the team. Further, the plan should specify a hierarchy, or communication chain protocol. When a crisis hits, your team's reaction should be like a pit stop in a NASCAR race. Every stakeholder should know his or her role and take immediate action. There should be a preplanned protocol for each action.

Depending on the size and scope of the crisis, the team should have the ability to assemble within the hour. But each classification of crisis should have a distinct course of action. The team members should practice their skills periodically to keep roles and responsibilities crisp and clear.

There are several essential elements of a plan that may not be readily obvious. Some of them will be extremely easy to complete and should have the status of "Just do it."

The Media Is No Friend of Business

There is a significant risk that the media might become involved while you are in the throes of a crisis. You should assume that the media will see every action you undertake in the most negative light. To put it more simply, the media will not be your ally in a crisis. The public loves to hate business people, and the media is a willing facilitator. As such, each employee (except the company spokesperson) should be advised not to speak to the media under any circumstances. The media policy should be part of a broader code-of-conduct plan that is signed by every employee.

Another useful – and necessary – tactic is a no-recording-equipment policy. Signs should be prominently posted at each of your locations that clearly state that the company has a policy prohibiting video or audio recording on the property.

With that policy in place, you can avoid having the media enter your place of business with cameras or recording devices. The media cannot even set foot on your property with their equipment.

As part of your crisis plan, you should have a company spokesperson. He or she can either be an employee or a retained professional. Also, you should designate at least one additional spokesperson, in the event that the primary spokesperson is unavailable. You may even choose to have multiple spokespeople who would assume the role in specific situations. For example, it might be the human resources professional who would speak on behalf of the company for employee-related issues, or a head research scientist who would comment on product performance issues.

Regardless of how you choose to proceed, you should have each spokesperson or potential spokesperson go through media training. Media training is a straightforward and relatively inexpensive investment and will easily pay for itself during the first crisis. You will also learn if your spokespeople have what it takes to effectively represent the organization.

During a crisis, you absolutely cannot afford a public relations gaffe. Such a misstep will only exacerbate the situation. So, having people who can weather the tactics of the media during a crisis is extremely important. And for serious crises, engagement of a public relations professional to coach your spokespeople through interviews is a requirement. Preparation for interviews and press conferences should include the use of mock questions and rehearsed answers.

In most cases, when the media contacts your organization, it is best to secure their call-back information and then return their call promptly after you have had a chance to prep your spokesperson.

The worst thing you can do is allow someone to speak to the media without an agreed-upon company position. Almost as problematic is to not respond to media inquiries. Failing to respond will irritate the media; they will come to their own conclusions. They will portray your non-response with a negative implication, as, "We attempted to contact the company, but they did not return our calls."

With the advent of the internet, an uncontrolled crisis has the potential to become a worldwide maelstrom in minutes. For this reason, another element of your crisis planning program should be the daily review of the internet. The internet should be scoured for any stories involving the company name, brands, facilities, or key leaders. This task is easily completed by preparing Google Alerts; or, you can also hire a company to provide the service.

Book 1 Leadership: The Responsibility to Ignite

Either way, a business simply cannot afford to have the world know about bad press before its own owners and executives do. Far too many companies have buried their heads in the sand and refused to understand the implications of an online world – with disastrous results.

A Crisis Playbook Is a Vital Tool

More extensive planning would include the creation of a crisis playbook. It will outline each step of the process for each type of crisis. The playbook should be prepared with the involvement of all key stakeholders, and it should be revised each year to include current information. Communication tree contacts and key staff members often change roles, and the plan should be updated at those times as well.

A bit more difficult to execute – but also worthy of consideration – is a contingency planning protocol in the event of a major, unexpected event. Most companies fail to plan for these types of crises and are forced into a scramble mode when disasters occur.

Often, you can work with others in your industry (who may not be direct competitors) to have a catastrophic planning reciprocity agreement. Such agreements will offer a degree of normalcy when a crisis hits.

I think about business – particularly during a crisis – as an algebraic equation that requires our best thinking to find the answer we seek. As in algebra, the more variables in play, the more complicated the solution. There is an algebraic principle that has us hold variables constant to facilitate solving for X. Business is no different. When a crisis occurs, holding as many controllable outside factors constant as possible allows the team to focus on the actual issue: solving for X, with X being the crisis.

FIRESTARTER

Holding variables constant is important, so that the team does not chase red herrings. The team should quickly focus on and define the scope of the crisis. Using the communication tools and protocols outlined in Chapter 4 will help bring a sense of normalcy to the crisis. Employing the proper tools will allow the team to get to the solution as efficiently as possible.

A few simple rules to help resolve current crises and prevent potential future problems are:

1. Make sure your receptionist and others who greet people are well trained on identifying phone calls or visitors who might cause a potential issue.

    a. Make sure they have a keen sense of how to respond to questions and know how to contact the appropriate personnel immediately.

2. Conduct the same training with all your consumer affairs personnel.

3. Educate your entire team on the perils of leaking company information to the outside world.

4. In most instances, the details of a crisis should be known only by a very small team of people, and great care should be taken to ensure that confidence and communication is held tightly.

5. During larger crises, especially if they become widely known to the public, clearly communicate the company's message to the entire team on a regular basis. Failing to do so will lead team members to engage in speculation. Speculation only leads to uncertainty and will fuel the crisis.

6. Insist that crisis team members limit discussions about the event to formal meetings. Also insist that information

in those meetings remain private, and that only approved company messaging leaves the room.

7. Request that all team members ask questions.
8. All rumors should be brought to the crisis team's attention.

During Crises, the Leader Must be Visible – But Stoic

When a crisis hits, the uncertainty that comes along with it tends to fuel fear. It is human nature to think about the worst outcomes. But as the leader, it is your responsibility to manage the fear factor. That does not mean deceiving team members; it means shouldering the responsibility and the risk, as appropriate for the circumstances.

Fear leads to panic, and when panic ensues, all control is lost. At that point, the crisis can become a wildfire. Remaining unemotional – while demonstrating your sincere concern – will speak volumes to the team around you. It is your job to guide the team through the crisis.

Inevitably, someone on the team will take Chicken Little's "The Sky Is Falling" position. That can be a real challenge for you as the leader, and you simply cannot afford to allow that negativity to taint the team's attitude. At the same time, you cannot be seen as flippant or nonchalant about the risks facing the organization.

If a team member expresses panic in a meeting, I advise that you call a break and engage the individual, one-on-one. Explain that you are fully aware of the severity of the situation, and reassure them that their concerns will be addressed. Also, urge them to use a controlled tone and tenor in their voice, and to phrase their concerns in question form.

A leader should also be visible to team members during crises. A great model for visibility and composure is the character of Captain Kirk, as depicted on Star Trek. He was always at the bridge of the starship Enterprise during a crisis. He gave commands to the team around him in a calm manner, without ever sweating. Everyone on the ship – and everyone at home, watching the show – knew who was in charge. It should be the same way in business. The leader makes the calls, and he or she must make those calls deftly and calmly.

If the crisis becomes well known to the public, it is even more important that you are visible. In fact, you should make the effort to be seen throughout the operation or office to answer any questions that concerned employees might have. You should avoid getting into protracted discussions, but when the rest of the team sees that you are accessible, it will help pacify their fears.

As the leader, you are the key resource in minimizing the impact of a crisis. You are responsible for ensuring that your team members are used efficiently to resolve it. Remember, things are rarely as good or bad as they seem at the time. Keeping everything in perspective – while still preparing for the worst possible outcome – will usually generate the best results.

Uncontrolled Spontaneous Combustion

President Harry Truman was known for using the phrase, "If you can't stand the heat, get out of the kitchen." At times, crises seem to come out of nowhere. The heat can become unbearable. Those are the times when the leader's courage, discernment, and steadfastness will be tested. Every ounce of the leader's fortitude may be required to successfully traverse the flames.

In March 2007, the companion animal industry was caught flat-footed. A report surfaced that dogs and cats were dying because their food was tainted. Concerned consumers' calls flooded pet nutrition companies' customer care lines beyond capacity.

Book 1 Leadership: The Responsibility to Ignite

I'd been working in the industry for over much of three decades and I had never seen anything quite like it. Full-scale consumer panic ensued. After a few days, reports began suggesting that there was rat poison in the food. The media was relentless – and the industry had no answers.

Almost immediately, our team expanded the resources and hours within our consumer affairs team. None of our products were specified, but we made sure that consumers' fears were quelled. We enacted an almost 24/7 approach. A consumer seeking answers could talk to a live person on our team at any time. Every person who answered the phone was thoroughly trained. We appeared to be keeping most consumers happy.

We soon discovered that an ingredient, sourced from China, was tainted. That ingredient was so widely used in the industry that nearly every one of our competitors was impacted. We found ourselves in a fortunate position, as we had not sourced the ingredient from that supplier.

Matters got worse. Because the industry regularly blended products from different formulations, even brands that were initially spared from the crisis soon found themselves involved. The uncontrolled crisis fire became an inferno as many consumers lost faith in brands they had trusted for decades.

While my company never had any products that were directly affected, there was one product that we jointly produced with a different supplier; that particular supplier discovered that some of their batches were tainted. Because the consumer would see no discernable difference between our batches (other than by looking at the production code), we prepared for a tidal wave of calls.

It was Easter weekend; sure enough, our call line was flooded. It got so intense that even our VP of Marketing took a turn fielding calls from frightened consumers. As it turned out, the other supplier did not see the need to enhance their call line and had failed to staff it adequately.

It was not an ideal situation, but we made it through that weekend unscathed. We logged over 1,000 calls, and handled each one with professionalism and empathy. I was proud of our team, and pleased that the crisis program had worked.

For the industry as a whole, the crisis involving the imported tainted ingredient delivered an almost-fatal blow to consumer confidence. It took years to rebuild trust with the consumers, but we did it.

After the Crisis, the Real Work Begins

Once a crisis is over, of course, everyone breathes a huge sigh of relief. But that is the time when the leader must push the team to the next level.

Team members – understandably – will be mentally exhausted, and it will be natural for them to want to relax. However, the leader must guide the team to avoid that inclination and remind the members that the crisis is not truly resolved until a postmortem report on it has been completed.

For example, after the crisis I just described, our postmortem review determined that we had been more lucky than good. As a result, we redoubled our efforts toward crisis management planning and response.

Many leaders will advise waiting a few days before conducting the postmortem to allow team members to recharge. In my experience, doing that will have a couple of very serious adverse consequences.

First, people tend to quickly forget all the details of the crisis. Recording all the accurate information in a timely manner is

Book 1 Leadership: The Responsibility to Ignite

essential, so that you can prepare to deal with the next crisis. Better yet, information in the postmortem report may help you avoid the next crisis before it happens.

Second, if not done right away, the postmortem review tends to be put off and never completed.

The leader must have an innate sense of how far he or she can push the team. That way, even though each crisis will have its own unique sequence, the postmortem will be finished within a reasonable time frame. Failure to complete a postmortem is an invitation for failure. Some of the best lessons on how to handle a future crisis will come from completing a full and thorough review of the last crisis. The postmortem should include:

1. What was the root cause or causes of the crisis?
2. Have those root causes been eliminated or addressed?
3. What did the team do that was helpful?
4. What could the team have done better?
5. How can we improve our crisis team?
6. How do we learn from having gone through what we just did?
7. What learning can we apply to other facets of our business?
8. What action do we need to take now?
9. What action do we need to take in the future?

If we take the correct approach to crisis management, we can emerge stronger and more capable. Since each crisis has its own idiosyncrasies, results will vary. Your goal must be to minimize negative implications and maximize learning.

> I can't change the direction of the wind, but I can adjust my sails to always reach my destination.
>
> **– Jimmy Dean**

Sailing Into the Wind

To me, one metaphor that clearly illuminates what is needed in a crisis comes from sailing. When I was a young boy, my uncle taught me how to sail. He had an Albacore sailboat, which is remarkable in its scope of use – anyone from a novice to a skilled sailor can sail it. I marveled at the boat's ability to defy logic by sailing into the wind.

If you are a sailor, you know that – if controlled properly – it is easy for a sailboat to reach a destination that is directly upwind. However, it takes skill and patience to learn to accomplish that. Using a method known as tacking, the captain and crew can use the seemingly unfriendly weather conditions to their advantage. When tacking, you are navigating the boat in a zigzag pattern from port to starboard, and repeating the maneuver until you reach your destination. At no point are you moving directly towards the target, as the wind will not allow the boat to travel in that direction. I have applied this tacking metaphor to business in many circumstances. But it is especially appropriate to discuss here – navigating a business crisis could be considered much like sailing into the wind.

It's logical to presume that the fastest and best way between two points is a straight line. Unfortunately, factors like competition, adverse market conditions, or capital constraints rarely allow for a company to take that direct path. So, we must use tactics that will ultimately allow the team to achieve its goal, although they may appear to be counterproductive in the short term.

Scenario planning of how to sail into the wind is an important exercise for teams, because failing to understand the implications of each move creates confusion. That confusion can lead to chaos; or, at the very least, the team could question the leader's ability to make sound decisions. It should be explained to the team that the leadership has not lost their minds; they are simply intentionally "tacking to the port side," because conditions will not allow the team to move directly right away.

But then, as soon as the team gets used to the new direction, the leadership decides to "tack starboard." To add to the complexity in business, "weather conditions" can change rapidly when you "tack." You must be ready for any next "tack" that changing conditions might dictate.

In business tacking, it pays to prepare for the execution of multiple future tacks. And it is equally important to not become too invested in a tack that you might have taken. Remaining nimble – adaptable – will allow you a clear advantage.

Whether it is done during a crisis or not, a tack or two along the way will enhance the leadership journey. I cannot think of a single important endeavor in my business career that did not require this skill. In some cases, I was ready; other situations caught me by surprise. In many cases, I simply got lucky. When your team is healthy, you can make luck a reality that works for you. Then, no longer is luck a flip of the coin; rather, you have created your own coin with two heads – and you know the right call to make.

Lighthearted Lessons: It Takes Three

The Question

As part of my role with a large consumer products company, I was responsible for the supply chain for the tuna division. We encountered quite a few crises during my tenure, but one consumer call stands out.

We received a call from a consumer who had found a case of tuna in a dumpster. He was curious if it was safe to eat. "In a dumpster" and "completely safe" seem – at least on the surface – to be incongruent terms. Would the safety of the food depend on how far below the surface of the dumpster that the tuna was discovered?

Upon answering the call, our associate asked for the code date information on the can. He confirmed that the tuna was completely safe to eat. We had an amazingly well-trained staff; but in this case, we missed the bigger picture. Maybe we should have simply stated, "If the product is in a dumpster, you should not eat it."

Two Glasses of Water

In my time with the companion animal nutrition industry, we were days away from the launch of a new dog food product – a dental treat designed to freshen dogs' breath and clean their teeth – that we had developed for a customer. Suddenly, panic hit. A news report came out about a similar product made by one of our competitors. The competitor's product had killed a dog when the product was swallowed whole. It had not dissolved in the animal's digestive tract. The national newscaster described the problem in a TV broadcast, with the backdrop of a deceased pet's legs and feet protruding from an open freezer.

Complete chaos ensued. We had already produced millions of units in support of the initiative. It represented the largest product launch in the history of our company. I knew that our process was different from our competitor's, but we had no real scientific basis to prove it. For a short time, we considered scrapping the entire launch.

The team scrambled. We found a university that had an artificial canine digestive tract; however, testing of our product would take more than a week. The wait would be excruciating. But that evening I had an idea. Before bed, I placed the competitor's product in one glass of water and ours in another one. The next morning, I returned to the glasses and the competitor's product appeared unaltered, while ours had dissolved by about 30 percent. While my observation was not proof, it was encouraging.

I contacted the customer and shared the news. While we still had to wait for the official results, we all slept better that week. We even joked that if the city water was more acidic than a dog's digestive tract, we would have an even bigger problem.

The scientific tests came back, and our dental treats were deemed fully safe for canine consumption. I admit it – I ate one or two of them, and found them rather tasty.

David and Goliath

One of our factories was on the edge of a residential area. For years, the company had been facing public scrutiny for various issues that the neighbors found objectionable. Our response to their complaints was to purchase their homes; we did so for three of the residents. One difficult neighbor remained.

A crisis came with the Monday of Holy Week. The remaining nearby resident notified the media that, in protest of our company, he was going to build a "protest chamber" on his property and conduct a hunger strike until we addressed his issues.

The fact that all of the local authorities had granted approval of our operations was lost on him and on the media. The media ate it up, and I was faced with cameras and reporters demanding to know the company position. Fortunately, I was able to avoid them and turned their inquiries over to our outside public relations agency. Nevertheless, I still had to deal with this nut case; I scheduled a meeting with him and his wife. I offered to buy his home for fair market value, restating a standing offer that had been in place for years.

Realizing that his "protest chamber" was easier trumpeted to the media than constructed, he decided to accept our offer to buy the home.

Four months earlier, he had pretended to be wheelchair bound and was sitting in front of the local Walmart with a sign proclaiming that his Christmas wouldn't be merry, because my company's negligence had forced him into a life as an invalid!

By Maundy Thursday, the matter was resolved. Despite having successfully achieved the outcome that we had desired for years, the media found it acceptable to run a headline praising the "poor man" and his wife. The headline was "David Slays Goliath." I guess they were tying in a religious theme to the Easter Week debacle.

CHAPTER 7

It's a Great Fire, But...

Maybe the most any of us can expect of ourselves isn't perfection, but progress.

– Michelle Burford

Have you ever been exposed to a situation that did not seem to have an optimal solution? How did you respond? How could you have handled it more effectively?

We are all imperfect beings. Some of our imperfections can be debilitating, while others are just inconsequential quirks. Truly examining one's self and separating those imperfections that are meaningful from the ones that are not that important is rather enlightening. A good leader engages in continuous reflection, within a healthy perspective. In other words, it is not productive to obsess over our flaws; nevertheless, we should strive for improvement.

As I have continued through my leadership journey, I have tried to improve my skills, behaviors, and – most importantly – my response to constructive criticism and difficulties in general.

In the first few years of my career, I obsessed over criticism that I thought was unjust. I would agonize over how to defend myself against those cruel and unfair attacks. Sleepless nights fueled my anger, and I found myself spiraling down into unproductive and mentally unhealthy environments.

One of my career epiphanies came during a training session. I came to realize that criticism and attacks can be extremely helpful as character builders. Even attacks that turn out to be unwarranted can help us gain perspective.

But there are criticisms that are truly constructive in nature. We can have our eyes opened to blind spots in our character. Think about a time when you felt attacked, but something productive came out of it. What did you learn from the experience? What changes did you make to your approach as a result?

Early on, I was known as a counter-puncher. Any attack on me or my team would be met with an extreme response. My reactions were so outlandish that many feared my rebuke. Since most of the attacks were emotional tirades, my fact-based retorts left my opponents reeling. And then, I would pile on, leaving my victim cowering.

I recall the aftermath of one such fiery exchange. I simply smiled broadly at the beaten spirit and asked a question that became noted in company lore. "When are you going to learn never to take me on?"

Another memorable dialogue came when an associate threw a set of keys at me and remarked, "If you want to drive the bus, then here are the keys."

My response became almost legendary: "At least someone who knows how to drive has them."

A New Perspective

Looking back, I now realize that while it felt good to be victorious in the moment, my approach brought on some long-term challenges. I unwittingly created relational conflicts that exacerbated the situation and stifled any potential for future collaboration. Worse, I set an example for my team members that was less than inspiring.

It's important to realize that there are times when such draconian conduct might be warranted. But when it becomes one's default position, it can result in lost opportunities. It flies in the face of organizational cooperation, and without optimized cooperation, the company cannot perform well.

At the same time, every company, every leader, and almost everything we touch is perceived in a certain way. Take, for example, onions. They are known to add flavor to a variety of recipes. They can be eaten alone or integrated into a multi-ingredient dish. They can be enjoyed both raw or cooked. It's fair to say that they are, by most accounts, a great addition to many recipes.

There is another side to the onion – a less appealing one. While their flavor and aroma can be a positive addition to recipes, onions also can create bad breath, gas, or abdominal discomfort. Simply cutting and preparing onions can burn the eyes and nose, causing tears. We find those attributes less desirable.

We could make the following statements about onions: "Onions are a delicious addition to salads and soups. They provide excellent flavor, but when I eat them, I get bad breath and become gassy."

In a nutshell, there is almost always a "but" in every description. When we look at people and companies, we regularly see that same qualifier. An example might be: "Company X makes a great product, but it's not a good place to work." Another might be: "Company Y is a great place to work, but their products are not of good quality." Like it or not, there is a "but" in your company's reputation. There is also a "but" in your image.

I have used this reality to create a training session titled *After the But*. Through an examination process, we uncover everything that could be viewed as a negative attribute. We might learn of those attributes through partner surveys or employee surveys. Or we might even stop into a local bar and listen to what the townspeople think about us.

Once we have gathered all the data, we can segment it. We can list all attributes and note those that appear to be real impediments to an optimized organization. Other qualities on the list, however, might be marked as inconsequential.

An example of a foundational issue might be a widespread perception that the company is a poor place to work. To address that, we can first ask why people might feel that way. Some views might stem from very basic beliefs. Others' beliefs might be far more complicated.

Conflicting Priorities

One company hired me to help them enhance their image. There was a perception that the company was a bad place to work, and the level of pay was a major factor in that view. However, my investigation revealed that the company's health-related benefits were far more generous than any of its peer companies. So generous were those benefits that the company was prepared to offer employees a $1-per-hour pay increase if the employees would approve a change to a less-generous health plan. Problem solved, right? Not so fast – many of the employees loved the benefit structure, and the thought of losing those benefits was troubling to them.

The two sides of the issue made for a seemingly unsolvable dilemma, until the company began to think outside the box. A two-tiered health-care benefit system was born. All employees were given a $1-per-hour increase in their base wages; the new pay scale included a trimmed-down health-care plan. However, employees were able to choose additional benefits, if desired, and fund them with their $1-per-hour wage increase. The fact that the government allowed contributions to medical benefit plans to be taken from pretax dollars created a very desirable outcome.

The impact to the company's financial situation was a net positive. True, the $1-per-hour wage increase impacted the costs of overtime, but the new wage structure significantly enhanced employee retention rates. The pay increase made recruitment efforts much easier, and the company's reputation soared in the community. Some of the money that had been budgeted on retention and onboarding could be redeployed to other, more productive, endeavors.

Image Is Important

Whether we admit it or not, people are drawn to companies and people who have a positive image. The attraction becomes contagious. As an example, there are two major grocers who compete in the town where I live in the summer: Tops and Wegmans. Both seem to attract different clienteles. I shop at both stores; but the Tops is closer to my home, so I shop there out of convenience. But Wegmans is a destination shopping trip. Within the community, their image is so robust that it's almost a social anomaly. They have created a perception of excellence, and they back it up with every aspect of their consumer experience. People rave about their visits to Wegmans.

Wegmans offers a full line of hard goods that are not normally found in other stores. They also boast a superior catering service and an impressive in-store restaurant. Wegmans wants you to enjoy your experience with them, and they even offer a day care facility for children while parents are shopping. The store associates are well paid and exceptionally trained. Wegmans is known as a great place to work.

All of the positive factors working in concert creates an enjoyable experience that is contagious. The results are happier shoppers and undeniable loyalty. It is not uncommon to see broad smiles on the faces of Wegmans shoppers.

Wegmans has marketed their image into a few taglines that clearly announce their intention for customers. Two that I like in particular are:

Helping You Live a Better Life Through Food
Discover Delicious

On the flip side, the Tops market offers similar services to those provided by Wegmans, but it seems to miss the mark. For example, their lunch area is rarely populated. At the Tops, there might be one or two individuals having a coffee; meanwhile, at the much-larger Wegmans restaurant, it is often so busy that there is a line to get a seat.

The displays at Tops seem far less enticing, and they attract shoppers through sales that promote pantry loading. On the other hand, Wegmans rarely – if ever – offers products at a discount.

In the final assessment, the comparison could be best summed up this way: Shoppers shop at Tops because of need and economic incentive, but Wegmans shoppers go for the experience. Both models seem to work, yet the Wegmans attraction is so magnetic that even during economic downturns, their loyal shoppers continue to flock there.

Book 1 Leadership: The Responsibility to Ignite

Building Upon a Reputation

Let's return to an example of the *After the But* analysis. A qualifier or deterrent might be price. The sentiment might be: "I love everything about the product, but the price is too high." In that case, the company has a couple of choices. One option might be to trim some expenses and get the price down to a more acceptable one.

Another path might be to embrace a higher pricing structure and ensconce it in an image of luxury. A great example is the car industry. Historically, most automakers employed a "good, better and best" pricing strategy. In addition to its flagship brand, Ford also offered Mercury and Lincoln.

Mercury was a medium-priced, better version of Ford. Lincoln was the luxury car, or a 'best offering' in Ford Motor Company. However, during the financial crisis of 2008, many of the long-standing, medium-priced automobile brands disappeared; the differentiation was unsustainable.

I own both a Ford and a Lincoln. The vehicles are similar, but the Lincoln includes a few elements that add up to a more luxurious, overall experience. I paid nearly double for my Lincoln than I did my Ford. To me, it is undeniable that the extra bells and whistles that came with the Lincoln were not really worth the extra expense. So, to examine the purchase through an economic lens, the Lincoln was a poor decision.

But I love my Lincoln; and I would make the same buying decision again. Interestingly, the marketing group at Lincoln is acutely aware of customer preference and embraces it throughout all of its brand-building initiatives. "Find Your Sanctuary" is a recent Lincoln tagline.

The final question becomes: Are Lincolns overpriced? The answer is, yes. The next question becomes: Is that of any consequence? The answer is, no.

What Does 'Good' Look Like?

So many times, company teams get so caught up in conducting day-to-day business that they fail to recognize that they should be on a journey toward excellence. They have never contemplated what will happen when they arrive at the journey's end or why they even chose the destination.

My current roles in business are either as a consultant or as an outside board member. One of the most interesting aspects of each of these roles is that I have a very different perspective than the team members who live their work experiences every day. Motivations aside, when I am engaged in a meeting, I find that team members have poured a tremendous amount of effort toward creating detailed, perfectly-presented analyses. But what about the content?

In a meeting, I will regularly ask about the target, or what the team sees as a successful outcome. The response that I usually receive is a look of confusion, followed by an explanation about how the company is improving.

Yes, clearly, the information provided demonstrates that an improvement has been made. But then I will follow up with a question about the company's ability to improve further. There is likely to be a general response that there is room to improve. At that point, I will ask how much improvement is possible… and confusion ensues.

Finally, I will ask a question that better illustrates my point. "What does 'good' look like?" I ask, followed by, "And how do you know when you are there?"

How is your business doing? Can you improve? By how much? How long should it take? How long will it take?

All of these questions should be followed with: How do you know? Why is it important?

Book 1 Leadership: The Responsibility to Ignite

What About You?

As we have discussed, companies have reputations; but, so do we. What does yours look like? Have you thought about the "after the but" when it comes to you and your image? Let's face it, we all have shortcomings. Those are the "after the but" characteristics that are viewed by most as negative – or at a minimum, suboptimal. Many people go through life unaware of their shortcomings. Or, maybe they are not curious enough to explore them.

If you are trying to become the best version of the leader that you can become, then you must constantly be on the lookout for your own negative traits. You can train yourself to minimize them. For example, I tend to talk over people and not take the time to listen. It is a trait that I work on, tirelessly. Still, I find myself interrupting and pontificating. As with many people, that particular behavior becomes more pronounced when I am passionate about a topic.

When I realize that I'm interrupting, I try to correct my behavior right away. I apologize to the other parties involved and allow them to finish their thoughts. It ends up being a bit awkward, and I continue to work on controlling my proclivity to interrupt.

What I have found is that if I plan for the conversation, I can better control my behavior. My solution remains imperfect, but over time I have seen great progress. When I take the time to listen, I find that I learn much more than I otherwise would have.

What are your "after the but" characteristics? Have you focused on correcting the behaviors?

A Word About Perfection

It is important to note that no one living today is perfect. Similarly, no situation is perfect. There are gradients of goodness that can make a person's personality more positive. While perfection is unattainable, striving to become more perfect is a sound and admirable endeavor.

For five years, I worked for a man who was wickedly smart. He might have been one of the best financial minds I had ever seen. He was honest and dedicated. His "after the but" characteristic? He was a bully. He seemingly could not help himself. He cursed constantly, and was always engaging in some annoying bravado. He was disliked or feared by most in the company.

I loved working for him. I could mix up the salty language with him when required. Moreover, I realized that his bullying was a defense mechanism.

He and I would go toe-to-toe, but deep down, I think we both respected the other for the contributions we made to the team. Still, he and I could not have had two more different management styles.

One day, on a trip to a remote site, we were in a large meeting with around 20 members of the senior management team. My boss was struggling with a new boss of his own, who was a repellent individual. His stress resulted in less-than-admirable behaviors. In the middle of the meeting, this man tore my presentation in half, claiming it was garbage.

Rising to my feet, I advised him that I was not going to be subjected to such shabby treatment. I informed him that I was flying home.

He did not get angry; rather, he announced to the entire team that if Haverlack was leaving, he was leaving too. Before I knew it, we were all scrambling to get to the airport.

Deep down, I believe he knew he had been wrong, but he refused to admit it. He seemed to not care about his own image. I saw that his behavior was holding him back. Deep down, he was a great guy – but I was one of the only people who knew it.

When faced with a challenge, whether personal or environmental, we must seek to find the most perfect solution available to us – knowing, of course, that it will not be perfect. Opting for the least imperfect answer to a challenge will provide the most expedient and beneficial result.

As you continue your journey, ask yourself a few questions. What are my blindspots? Are there opportunities for improvement? What is the best approach to minimize my shortcomings? What is my "after the but?"

Lighthearted Lessons: Every Firestarter Has Flaws

Early in my career, I oversaw a fleet of commercial transport vehicles. The Teamsters union represented the drivers. The relations between management and the union were not so great. I worked hard to build trust with the drivers. For the most part, it worked, but on occasion there were some squabbles.

One driver repeatedly exhibited poor behavior and he would constantly lie about his performance. He and I came to an impasse, and I found myself in a mediation session with representatives from both the company and the union. Tempers began to flare.

An attack on my character threw me into a rage. I began to berate the driver in the most objectionable fashion. Part of my tirade included a question on how he could kiss his 10-year-old daughter as he tucked her into bed, knowing he was a liar.

My query evidently got to him. He began a complete admission of his dishonesty and gave a total accounting of his poor behaviors. But I didn't hear a word; I was caught up in emotion and continued with my attack. Finally, our HR lead physically restrained me, and informed me that the driver had confessed and accepted his punishment.

Interestingly, that driver then became one of my best. For all my faults, I am a rather empathetic soul, and when I realized how bad my conduct was, I publicly apologized to him. That apology marked a defining point in our personal relationship and in the overall relations with the other drivers.

Later in my career, I worked for a man who was an interesting character. He was a deeply religious man, and I never heard him utter a single curse word. Nevertheless, he exhibited some of the most abusive behavior I have ever witnessed.

As I have done with other superiors, I looked for the good in him, and overall we had a productive and positive relationship. However, he had a baseball bat in his office and he carried it around. Regularly, he would emerge from his office – bat in hand – and beckon me to join him.

I suspect that he had no clue that his practice of carrying the bat was humiliating and abusive. I was not alone; many of his other senior leaders suffered under his implied threat.

One day, after he beckoned with the bat, I said with a loud booming voice, "Not the face this time. Please, not the face!"

He was embarrassed; he and I entered his office laughing. To my knowledge, he never held that bat in his hand again. Other than calling me a knucklehead, he never mentioned the incident again.

He was also verbally abusive in meetings, criticizing almost every aspect of the work done by subordinates. One day, after enduring some of his extreme criticism, I announced that I agreed with him. I added, "You are right, I am a worthless piece of crap and I don't deserve to live."

The room became silent. My team members awaited my punishment. After an uncomfortable 30 seconds, he started laughing

Book 1 Leadership: The Responsibility to Ignite

uncontrollably. "What am I going to do with you?" he asked. I responded, "Love me."

A few weeks later, one of my cohorts tried the same stunt. My boss rebuked him, saying, "Only Haverlack is allowed to do that."

CHAPTER 8

Tending the Fire

Fire is never a gentle master.

– **Proverb**

During the time that this book was in its final stage of creation, wildfires were raging across the United States and Canada. One morning, I awoke to a thick haze that eerily enveloped my community. I quickly learned that the smoke from forest fires burning more than 1,000 miles away had impacted much of the eastern US. The far-away fires had rendered the air near my home unhealthy to breathe.

How fascinating, yet terrifying, I reflected.

There is nothing more terrifying than a fire out of control. It is exactly the same for leaders. Igniting, fueling and refueling a fire to create an inferno is exhilarating. However, there is the important work of tending the fire to ensure that we control the fire – instead of it controlling us. Successful leaders know that the work of nurturing the team is both essential and immensely rewarding.

This book is focused on nurturing. I hope you did not miss that. (I realize that it was probably easy to become distracted when you were engulfed by exciting text describing combustion.) The fact is that nurturing is one of the leader's primary responsibilities. Nurturing is necessary to keep all aspects of team dynamics productive. Being a nurturer requires knowing many of your teammates on a personal and vulnerable level.

But first, we must know ourselves. Forty-two years after my first leadership position, I continue to hone my skills. What kind of a leader am I? I suppose I am the leader I was meant to be – perfectly imperfect.

My personality type is ESTP (Extrovert Sensing Thinking Perceiving). As such, I am prone to become excited. My excitement fuels passion; and before I know it, I have reached the point of zealotry. Since I know that I have these tendencies, I also know that I must be ever-vigilant. So, I perform gut-checks on myself. Have I pushed too hard? Am I still on the path? Have I lost my way? Do I even know where I am? These are all questions I must ask myself on a regular basis.

What is your personality type? Learn it. Study it. Embrace it. Depending on your personality makeup, you might ask questions like, "Did I push hard enough?" "Is this path the right one?" "Is this where I am supposed to be?"

What about your team? What are their preferences? How can their unique personality types enhance team dynamics? What are their shortcomings? How can you help them overcome them?

The Moral Compass

One of the biggest risks facing the leader is temptation. Success fuels the ego – and while a robust ego is essential, an over-inflated one can set an out-of-control wildfire that can quickly destroy everything. A lifetime of accomplishment can be reduced to a smoldering pile of embers in an instant.

I have lived in a world of private jets and limousines. I have even had staff members who were responsible for washing my car and retrieving my dry cleaning. Having such luxuries can become so ingrained in your psyche that part of your identity can unexpectedly be lost if they are removed.

Our own moral compass can serve as a vital waymaker to help us remain grounded. The moral compass is that life-guiding internal document that enables us to commit our driving force to our core values. The moral compass is essential as we build the foundation of our lives. Don't have your moral compass calibrated? It's never too late to create this crucial navigation tool.

I had the great fortune to be born into humble beginnings. While I did not fully appreciate the struggles my family faced until I reached adulthood, I have grown to realize just how vital that perspective has been for me.

In our ever-evolving life journey, we become influenced by our experiences. Those influences can be both productive and unproductive. It is important to keep a recording of our journey, so that we can look back and realize how far we have come.

We must also ask ourselves some vital questions. Do we currently find ourselves more aligned with our moral compass, or less aligned with it? This vital waymaker is a game changer. Embrace it and allow it to guide you all the days of your life.

My Fiery Waterloo

In 2009, the company I led had become so successful that we simply could not keep up with the burgeoning demand. Profits were soaring, as was our image. We had become the talk of our industry. We had catapulted from a minor entity to the sixth largest member of our industry on the world stage.

Looking back, I can see that there were red lights flashing everywhere. But the blinders of success left me unable to see them. Before I knew it, I was the featured speaker at a press conference addressing the media, with the governor of Arkansas cheering me on. He and I crowed about the dozens of jobs that were to be created as part of our acquisition of a business in a remote part of the state.

The champagne overflowing from the crystal vessels seemed to be endless and the celebration roared on for over a year. A business that had grown more than tenfold over the previous decade was on the cusp of doubling again.

What could go wrong?

Well... I could opine about the failures of my team members, but the fact remains that as the president of the company, the responsibility started and stopped with me. In the final assessment, we lost more than $20 million; and worse yet, the chaos left much of the team confused and wandering aimlessly through the charred remains. The fire we set had blazed out of control... and it burned us.

In the final assessment, we were able to extinguish that destructive inferno. We set new, controlled fires that warmed up our business; but it took years for the company to fully recover. However, some personal burn damage could not be healed, and I announced my retirement in 2012. My successor leader, who had been sourced, prepared, and coached by me, finally overcame the turmoil. The company continued its trajectory of success, stoked by fires that were ignited during my tenure.

Tending My Personal Fire

Throughout my journey, I have found tools that have been extremely helpful in keeping the fire within me both stoked and controlled. My driving force comes from my love of God, love of country, and love of family. On top of that, I am driven by the love of winning. But more importantly, I revel in seeing the delight on the faces of others who have achieved something they thought was not possible.

In my office there is an array of memorabilia that reminds me of who I am, of my driving force, and of where I came from. There are more than 100 items... many relate to my career triumphs and tragedies. Included is an antique fire nozzle from a factory we revitalized in the 1990s. It was one of six presented during a celebration. Interestingly, it was given in recognition of my ability as a world-class firefighter.

Also included is artwork from my children created more than 30 years ago. There is a framed bag of M&Ms, reminding me that margin and mix are vital to every business. There is a picture of a shark, with the tip of a fishing rod attached. I broke that rod over the shark's head when I thought it was about to eat me.

Most significantly, there are a dozen Bibles, owned by various members of my family over the past nearly 200 years. And I'm surrounded by pictures of many of my ancestors and relatives, along with related mementos that commemorate their achievements, and their efforts in taking up arms against evil. Finally, on my desk are pictures of my wife, my children, and my granddaughter. They watch over me, in good times and bad. They remind me about what is important. They reassure me that the fires continue to burn brightly, and that every fire set was worth the effort.

FIRESTARTER

What is your driving force? How do you tend your personal fire? What does good look like in your world?

> Instead, whoever wants to become great among you must be your servant, and whoever wants to be first must be your slave, just as the Son of Man did not come to be served, but to serve, and
> to give His life as a ransom for many.
>
> **– Jesus of Nazareth, the Son of God**

Who better to send us on our journey than the greatest firestarter who has ever lived? When we reflect upon what Jesus accomplished – in less than three years – it leaves us utterly speechless. With none of our modern tools available, His message swept the world. Over 2,000 years later, the fires He ignited are burning brighter and more broadly than ever before.

Jesus was the embodiment of every characteristic we look for in a leader. He was humble, empathetic, courageous, and a great communicator. He was a visionary – most likely the most audacious visionary in history. His integrity is without question; and His discipline in spending 40 days in the wilderness is astounding. His message of optimism was shared impartially, resulting in much criticism from those in power.

Jesus took the ultimate risk, and did so for all of humanity. His ability to both educate and become educated are widely chronicled in the historical record. Simply stated, He is the greatest teacher to ever walk the earth.

He excelled at the important roles of a leader. He was a coach, a simplifier, and He had a curious, inquisitive nature. Let's examine coaching. There are six times when Jesus overtly coached the disciples.

Book 1 Leadership: The Responsibility to Ignite

My favorite was when he instructed Peter to put down his sword in the Garden of Gethsemane. He knew what awaited him; yet, he had the courage to coach Peter one last time.

Was Jesus curious? The vast majority of the questions posed to Jesus that are recorded in the Bible were answered with a question. That might be the definition of curiosity. His time in the Temple as a child, absorbing the law, is another great example of his curiosity and his zest for education. Jesus was also the great simplifier. He distilled the law down to a few verses:

> Love the Lord your God with all your heart
> and with all your soul and with all your mind.
> This is the first and greatest commandment.
> And the second is like it:
> Love your neighbor as yourself.

A measure of a great leader is his or her legacy... especially if the leader has helped create other good leaders. Part of Jesus' legacy is the transformation of His disciples – everyday men – into the most compelling leaders of their day. And even today, many of our best leaders are followers of Jesus.

What type of leader will you become? What will be your legacy? Who will you inspire? How many lives will you touch? Will the world be better for you having been born? These questions may challenge you; but becoming a leader is no easy feat. But being a leader can provide the most rewarding experience of your life. It might even be an essential part of your life's purpose.

If you are looking for power, wealth, and fame, you should pass on the role of leader. The role will probably not suit you, and it certainly will not suit those who follow you.

If you believe that becoming a leader will take you down the path that will enable you to become the best version of yourself, then go for it. Wealth, power, and fame might come with it – and if they do, so be it.

When you are successful, whether it is on a large platform or a smaller one, what you do with that success is vitally important. I believe that what we do when we win defines us, and becomes our legacy. Successful leaders give back. How much? The answer is simple – As Much As You Can.

So, it's decision-making time. The choice is yours. Choose wisely.

Go Forth... and Ignite!

BOOK 2

Leading Teams

The proper definition of a man is
an animal that writes letters.

~ Lewis Carroll

Letters that Burn

During my career, I have been blessed to lead some extraordinary teams. As early as 1981, I learned that my style should include **being real** with my teams.

In my parlance, **being real** means connecting with the teams in a very personal fashion. I believe that I have led well over 10,000 people in my 40-year career. Until it became impossible to do so, I learned every employee's name as well as the name of their spouse. When there were company functions, I made sure that I greeted the spouses by name.

I also worked to ensure that every employee knew I was a team player, and I made a good effort to participate in every job that I assigned an employee to do. I also let my employees know that I deeply appreciated their commitment to the company and to me. That meant thousands of hand-signed greeting cards and letters, hundreds of lunches, and nearly 100 celebrations. It also included my attempts at learning how to drive a tractor-trailer and trying to **uncouple** twin sets of trailers. For those who do not know about **uncoupling**, it requires an exceptional level of expertise – an expertise I did not possess.

My approach paid big dividends; my teams always seemed to outshine the competition. Even in one of my earliest jobs, I looked for areas to align with employees and create a genuine understanding.

The venue was an old bakery that had been a landmark of Pittsburgh for generations. But the environment was toxic, with management harboring a genuine dislike for the labor force. The labor force, in turn, did not trust management. It was much like a battleground, with two warring tribes bent on destroying each other. Predictably, the company suffered because of the conflict.

After some years with the company, I earned the privilege of leading the sanitation department. The department was comprised of uninspired, bottom-of-the-seniority-list "problem children." And, management had created the most unthinkable schedule for us; one that was the most onerous that the union contract would allow.

Very little was expected from my group, and as one might imagine, very little was produced by them. It was a true paradox – the people in arguably the most important role in the company, that of ensuring the food was safe to eat, were treated the most shabbily. Moreover, if the production team was short, an employee or a person was taken from the sanitation crew to fill the vacancy.

Shortly after taking on the assignment of leading the team, I studied the situation and devised a plan. It would require union buy-in, but would deliver a cleaner facility and safer products while creating far better working conditions. The plan called for eliminating the 24 full-time crew positions and creating 10 new, better jobs. The plan also included a part-time or shared employee pool that would work only when production was not operating, allowing for more deep cleaning. On the days when the part-time team members were not needed on the sanitation crew, they would be available for work in another department.

As one might imagine, the initial feedback from the union was unfavorable, to put it mildly. But their position softened after I revealed the entire plan. Consensus was reached, and within a few days, the new crew of 10 was intact. Among them was the head shop steward – who loved his new assignment – and nine others, all near or at the top of the seniority list.

Better people and enhanced working relationships resulted in immediate success. Once the worst department in almost every category, the sanitation team became the best in the company. We led statistically in almost every category.

Safety, a vital factor, might have been the most amazing component. We simply stopped having accidents. In turn, I rewarded the team with increased incentives. Five minutes added onto a break one day led to me cooking breakfast for the team... and that led to steaks grilled on the roof. We went three years without a single accident, and we broke every sanitation record in the industry.

At that time, a group known as the American Institute of Baking was an independent auditor. It was widely assumed that our 100-year-old facility could not deliver results that would reach the auditor's pinnacle of achievement – the Superior rating. Yet, within two years, the Superior flag flew over the company. I was asked how we pulled it off.

I simply never bothered to tell my team that it was impossible. I had great people who believed that it could be done, and they delivered the undeliverable. Moreover, I worked side by side with them every day (breaking a sacrosanct union rule), and they loved me for it. In turn, I loved them, and in every action, I made sure they knew how much.

My next challenge was working with the Teamsters union. The history of dealing with them was like a chapter from a horror story.

One of my predecessors had been beaten so badly by one of the union members that he never returned to work. I was not yet 30, and I would be the youngest to ever lead the group. It was a daunting task.

Trouble began with threatening calls to my home at night. I also found my car packed with garbage. Yet, within two years, before I was reassigned, my car would be filled with cases of beer by a team of professional drivers who had grown to respect me. I grew to respect them too.

Simply stated, we found ways to achieve win-win solutions to decades-long problems. I had found in my research that the drivers had been treated very shabbily by management; they responded by engaging in skullduggery to disrupt operations. As I spoke with the drivers individually, I found that they hated their own actions – but they felt that the behavior was necessary to keep the playing field equitable.

I learned that among our ranks were seven long-term drivers who had driven a combined **sixteen million miles** without an accident. The most senior driver had driven **four million miles,** accident free. And management had not said as much as a **thank you!** I remedied that by hosting a lavish rewards banquet, and I even invited a representative from the national Teamster organization to join me in recognizing our valiant stewards of safety.

Along with enhanced relations came improved performance. We cut cost-per-mile indices by more than 40 percent, and I personally rewarded each driver for their efforts.

One Good Friday, after an unexpected heavy snowfall had blanketed the area, I developed a plan. I knew that the team would find a way to make every delivery on time and return safely, and they did not disappoint me. I greeted each driver as they returned from their route and thanked every one with an Easter ham. It was a 16-hour-day for me, but worth every minute.

I adopted the same kind of philosophy in every assignment that I ever had. It has never failed me.

Some 30 years later in my career, I was presiding over a company and our summer picnic had over 500 in attendance. The company that had been hired to grill the food failed miserably; it was a near disaster. But to the delight of the attendees, I was able to jump in and man the grill, and deliver the hot dogs and hamburgers to the hungry crew. My stellar team of executives joined me and made the task an easy one.

My father always said, "You are no better or no worse than anyone else. When you start to believe you are superior, you have lost your way." **Being real** means connecting with other people at a personal level. It is the right thing to do.

I love writing. I do not consider myself a particularly unique wordsmith, but I write from the heart. Over my career, I have written hundreds of letters to my teammates. Most have been lost to history, but with the advent of computers, many from the last quarter-century have been saved. What follows is a selection of those letters.

LETTER 1

Everyone Wants to Win, But Will They

Everyone wants to win. I engaged in a furious debate with an individual last week about this very topic. His position was that my view was myopic and based only in the fact that I want to win. He insisted that winning to him was unimportant. While it is true that I do indeed like to win, I hold that everyone likes to win. Each person's definition of winning may be slightly different, but the fact that winning is core to human nature is hard to dispute.

This year we are winning like never before. You will hear statements like "record performance," "record pace," and "record breaking." All of these statements can be used to describe the first half of 2009 here. With the success comes excitement and celebration, all of which is exhilarating and invigorating.

Winning over the long term is the true definition of success. What we do today will determine the likelihood of future successes. Think of all the sports figures in history who made it big for one year only to fall short later. Instead of remembering them for their success, they are referred to as a "flash in the pan" or "underachiever." History can be quite cruel.

FIRESTARTER

At this company we are building a foundation on which we can build a long-term winning enterprise that will stand the test of time. It starts with investment in people, brands, relationships, and infrastructure and ends with a sustainable business model that will win in good times and bad ones.

We are committed to the education and development of our existing family members and the attraction of new people to help support this very different world in which we now compete. Education in food safety is of paramount importance and it must remain our primary focus.

We are investing in brands to create equities that will appeal to our target consumer base. Our endeavor with Rachael Ray is a recent example of this long view of brand building with more to come in the future.

Customer intimacy is our strategic anchor. For 76 years our name has been synonymous with great customer service and we are going to build on this heritage and take relationship building to the apex of the industry.

Finally, our investment in infrastructure and facilities has been a regular diet here, and MEP and our major investment in a state of the art baking entity are but two major examples. Expect to see more in the future. We are going to be more discerning than we have in the past by expecting notable wins in conjunction with future capital investment.

This type of investment and commitment, coupled with superb execution, speed and candor, is a powerful combination. We march toward the second half of 2009, and the years to come, with a potent arsenal confident that we can and will win. More importantly, a strong appetite for victory fuels our passion.

So last week, I argued my point and he argued his and after a 45 minute debate I finally gave in and my adversary seemed gratified. I ended the argument by simply stating "You Win." His response was "Oh Yeah."

LETTER 2

Live Our Values Everyday

It sure is exciting times. In the midst of economic uncertainty in our country and the world, this company's business continues to thrive and grow. This is great news for all of us. Along with this success has come a number of challenges and hurdles to overcome.

I know that many of you are working extremely hard and I appreciate your commitment to our organization. It is easy, when we are working hard and become tired, to forget where we are heading and the road we are traveling. In these times we have to be mindful to Live Our Values Everyday. It is no surprise that this creates the acronym L.O.V.E.

I think it is time for a whole lot of LOVE – a four-letter word we can all embrace but oftentimes feel uncomfortable using in the workplace. Wouldn't it be wonderful if we could hear more about love?

It is love that drives us. We love our families so we come to work to give them a better life. We love to do those things that we enjoy so we try to make time to do them. Hopefully, you all love your job as I love mine. I love to win. I make no excuses for it and I am not embarrassed by my feelings. We are winning and it is absolutely wonderful.

During the winning we need to address many challenges. We must remember to treat each other with respect and honesty, embrace change, be the best team player we can be, and recognize the needs of our customers both internally and externally. Along with this we must continue to look toward the long view.

We are aggressively working to expand our capacity in order to get our dedicated family members some much needed time off and to return to the stellar service level that has been the hallmark of this great enterprise. We have secured additional volume from another company who has been certified by our Food Safety team and we have entered into a long-term contract to expand our operations in Kansas. Bottom line – Help is on the Way.

Again, I want to thank all of you for your contributions. I ask you to remember to love each other and spread the love around.

LETTER 3

We Are Going Green

I am pleased to announce the creation of a formal sustainability initiative that is coming to our company in the very near future. As you are all aware we have participated in recycling efforts and energy efficiency programs for many years, but starting in 2009, we will be placing an emphasis on the environment like never before.

This effort will be led by Michael with Drew as the lead team sponsor of the program. They will be reporting progress directly to the Executive Team on a regular basis. These guys have done their homework and are real pros when it comes to understanding the key issues in the world of sustainability. It is safe to say "they bleed green."

The program will consist of an inward look at our processes and procedures with an outward look to trading partners, customers, and consumers. It will be an evolution that is intended to ultimately change the way we think about most everything we do.

We are in the process of assembling a cross functional team to direct the effort. We are looking for energetic participants who will help lead the charge. In fact, to make the most of the program we are asking every family member enterprise-wide to become an advocate for Green Living. Even the smallest change makes an impact and together we can all make a difference that we can be proud of while ensuring the best future for generations to come.

Please join me in supporting Michael and Drew as we roll out this program and in the months and years ahead as we invest in putting our entire family to work toward a cleaner and healthier world. We welcome any and all suggestions to help jump start the program. Stay tuned . . . . .

LETTER 4

Opportunity Knocks - We Will Answer

I attended the Global Pet Show in Orlando in late February and let's just say there were opportunities everywhere. The most overused terminology in 'show jargon' is "it was a great show." Well this time it really was a "great show." With at least ten tangible follow ups, it should be extremely exciting to see how things unfold.

Opportunity is constantly knocking, but will we answer? In order to answer we must be able to hear it. At times it is a loud thundering reverberation and easily recognized. Other times it comes in a light tap, almost inaudible, and in the hub-bub of life we fail to recognize its beckon. It's important that we make sure we are listening and hearing for opportunities at home and at work. A failure to answer the door may mean a significant improvement in our life's journey passing us by before we know it. Take time each day to reflect on what you have heard and encountered and determine what threads of opportunity might exist within them.

Once we understand which opportunities exist we must decide how we will answer. Questions to ask:

Is this opportunity right for us/me? *With 'us' being my family, friends or business.*

Can I turn this opportunity into a tangible result? *With a tangible result being happiness, friendships, new business, to name a few.*

Once we decide to accept the challenges that come when we bring an opportunity to fruition, we must turn our attention to flawless execution. Once standards are set at the apex and beyond expectations, success ensues.

As opportunities knock in your life make sure you hear, listen, answer, question and execute. As for our business, we are always ready to evaluate opportunities. If you hear a knock or a tap please communicate it. We have over 130 team members and nearly 300 extended team members at our affiliated companies poised and ready to join in the fun.

LETTER 5

Putting Points on the Board

As we close out 2006, I wanted to take a moment to thank you all for a fantastic overall performance. This year, working together as a team, we put points on the board like never before across our entire family of companies. We sold more, made more, and shipped more products than ever.

All three of our distinct company enterprises had record revenue years. Our quality systems, sanitation, and safety programs have all improved. Perfect scores on customer quality audits has become the standard and so has the Superior rating for AIB.

As we turn to the execution phase of the 2007 edition of our journey, I believe that our opportunities are vast and many and the challenges are more daunting. Like all great teams we need to focus on our respective roles and pay particular attention to the blocking and tackling that has brought us to this point.

I want to wish all of you and your families a safe and happy holiday season and prosperous and peaceful new year. 2007 is sure to be extremely exciting and I remain very confident that this team will score early and often to propel us to levels never before achieved.

LETTER 6

Tortilla Prices Triple – Facing Challenges

I was watching the news last week and there was rioting in Mexico because the price of tortillas have tripled in the past six months. Many of you are thinking 'the pressure must have finally gotten to him; what do tortillas have to do with pet food?'. The reality is there is quite a close comparison. The number one ingredient in tortillas is corn and that very same corn is the number one ingredient in many of the pet foods produced and sold in the United States.

Corn has almost doubled in price in the past six months and is currently trading at or above $4.00 a bushel. Unlike the tortilla market we cannot just simply pass these ingredient cost increases on to our customer. We are in an extremely competitive segment and as of this writing have had to absorb these increases and maintain our price points.

Sounds like trouble for 2007, you say. While the increased ingredient costs create a new challenge, it is one we can meet and overcome with the entire company family working together.

We can start by making more with less. With the advent of MEP and new high efficient dryers and extruders we are well positioned to improve our yield efficiencies and thus ensure that many more of the ingredients we mill and extrude make it to the consumer's pantry. In the interim and beyond, close control to specifications are key to ensuring we optimize our performance.

Many of the products we sell are only minimally affected by the increase in corn and other ingredient prices and we must drive more volume against these products. Driving sales on higher margin snack items, while we continue to focus on our full feeding diets is a great example of how to take advantage of the current economic realities facing our business.

There are dozens of things we can do working together to improve and drive cost savings. Everything, from watching the number of copies we make to keeping a close eye on the supplies we use, will all serve to help with belt tightening. We are all working very hard; but thinking about how to do things a little differently may very well take us over the top in 2007.

With one month in, 2007 looks to be another great year for our organization. Finding new ways to drive cost savings and drive incremental sales on the highest margin items will take us over the top. If you have a great idea, let's talk about it and see how to put it to work for all of us.

LETTER 7

Resolve to Be the Best

The new year is not even a month old and the experts tell us that 90% of New Year's Resolutions are already a distant memory. How are you doing with yours? If you are hanging in there great – keep up the good work; but you are definitely in the minority.

This year, instead of making a bunch of well-intentioned, but probably unachievable promises – despite your 'best' efforts you fail to keep and then "fall off the wagon" and wait for the calendar to turn another year to try again – let's resolve to live and work as our best self. We can start today.

The best part is we do not need to wait for the calendar to decide to make a change in our lives. One of my favorite sayings is "I can't do anything about what happened in the past but to learn from it" and so let's resolve to learn from past mistakes or "bad luck" and commit to do everything in our power to make the future better. If you stumble, determine what you can learn from the "fall" and start again smarter and better equipped to succeed.

Each of us has the unique ability to know ourselves. Setting small achievable goals often works best. For example, look at our QAKE audit record that has improved year after year. Our transformation did not occur overnight. It took years of hard work, training, and most importantly discipline. Today the guidelines of the QAKE audit are becoming a part of our daily life. While we earned a perfect score last year, true success comes when every day we employ the principles learned each and every day. Each day we improve and our goal is within reach.

Applying the attitude that "I can change what I desire to change" is extremely powerful. At home, at work, and at play resolving to be the best will pay huge dividends. Do not wait for next year or even next week. Start today.

LETTER 8

When Bad Things Happen

As I am sure you are all aware, our industry has been facing the biggest crisis in recent memory and maybe the largest in the history of the industry. Canine and feline sickness and death and, for what seemed to be an eternity, misinformation, and no real answers.

In a textbook case of media fueled panic, the fear of what is unknown precipitates rumors and misinformation. Toxins? Rat Poison? Melamine? As scientists race to find the root cause, companies debate the best course of action and consumers understandably scramble for answers.

The actions of the companies in the eye of the storm will be analyzed and debated long into the future. Questions like; *What could they have done differently?* And, *How could this have been avoided?* will be the topic of countless discussions in board rooms, classrooms, veterinarian offices and dinner tables across the United States and Canada.

While our company was not directly involved in the recall the implications and collateral ramifications have been stark. To date our company has logged over 5000 calls from concerned consumers.

I am pleased to advise you that our company and particularly our consumer affairs and quality assurance groups have been stalwart and professional in the handling of this crisis. A big "hats off" to all of them and to the other family members who have jumped in to help.

Directly involved or not, a crisis of this magnitude is not good for our industry. The most important questions for our company are: *What can we learn from this experience? What can we do to make sure we protect our company in the future?* and *What actions can we and the industry do to reassure a concerned consumer base?*

This crisis will become history and despite the current struggles our industry will be better and stronger for having experienced it. In business and in life crises happen and whether they are big or small, avoidable, or unavoidable they all have one thing in common: They are painful. How we handle them is the key to minimizing the pain.

LETTER 9

A Time for Thanks

Our industry continues to battle with the vestiges of a recall of unprecedented magnitude. Gasoline and diesel prices are at almost post Katrina levels. Ingredient prices continue to climb. These key issues could fill an entire newsletter, and as important as they are I felt it was more important to devote my article this month to say thanks.

Last month Big Brother and Big Sisters of Crawford County held its annual fundraiser, Bowl For Kids Sake. Thanks to the efforts of a great number of people the group exceeded its goals and raised over $88,000 to support mentoring programs for youth of our community. Our company family played a huge role in making this happen.

Our company family, a perennial supporter of Big Brothers and Sisters, contributed like never before. In an amazing demonstration of commitment and dedication our company family raised more money than ever and filled the lanes with more than twice the number of teams as last year.

As the President of the Board of BBBSCC for five years, I am truly gratified by the outpouring shown by our company family. I wanted you all to know how much I personally appreciate your commitment. As Chief Operating Officer, I could not be prouder of the way this family answered the call and your personal families jumped in and supported the effort as well.

Too often in our busy lives we forget to remember to thank people. It's not that we are not thankful, but so many issues crowd our lives that the niceties sometimes get lost. As such, a simple **Thank You** from the bottom of my heart is my message to you this month.

LETTER 10

We're In a Safety State of Mind

June is National Safety month and judging from the performance across all of our affiliated companies we have something to celebrate this year like never before. We are navigating new waters in safety excellence.

Our company and our sister enterprise in Warren, Pennsylvania, have maintained an accident free record through all of 2007 to date, and the Joplin, Missouri, team has vastly improved its performance as well and is currently on track to have its best year ever.

It is clear that safety has become one of our core competencies and is now woven into the fabric of our culture. I like to call it a *Safety State of Mind*. Achieving excellence in safety takes a great deal of dedication and commitment. Hats off to everyone working at all of our affiliated companies for such a fantastic effort.

Now that we have reached the *Safety State of Mind* the challenge is to keep it. Maintaining this status can be even more difficult than achieving it. Amongst the challenges is a continuous focus on how we conduct ourselves and to provide gentle reminders to our coworkers when they need them. Please remember we are on a mission and that only through a concerted effort from everyone will the team remain at the apex of performance.

Applying a *Safety State of Mind* to our home life is an additional challenge and one we often forget. The emergency rooms are full of people who made a "stupid mistake." Most of us have been there at least once in our lives. "I wish I had been more careful" echoes in our homes and when visiting with friends as pain and embarrassment fills our bodies and minds. So too the reality that we have jeopardized our livelihood and our families well being through perpetrating a seemingly innocent act gone wrong.

Applying a *Safety State of Mind* at work and at home is not always easy but it always pays huge dividends. Let's set a challenge to remain accident free for all of 2007 at work and at home.

LETTER 11

Staying in the Game

How many times have we seen or heard of a fantastic come back? A team is on the edge of elimination and they pull together and win. It's even more meaningful when an underdog pulls off the upset. In all of these cases two things remain constant. First, the team believed they could win and secondly, they remained in the game and continued to execute each play with the same passion and desire as the first. Had they given up or not believed they could win they most assuredly would have lost.

Business often parallels sports. The same passion and intensity that leads winning teams in sports offers vitally important fuel for success in business. 2007 has been an extremely challenging year. Run-away commodity prices, shrinking margins, and an unprecedented recall could be the headlines of 2007, and certainly have all contributed to less than optimal results thus far.

We are in the fourth quarter of an extremely challenging campaign, but what should not be lost in all the "bad" news is the fantastic positive progress we have made as a team.

FIRESTARTER

The headlines in 2007, include record revenues, stellar safety performance, a new best-in-class extrusion plant, stronger than ever relationships with key trading partners, several new exciting accounts on board, and a quality record that we can all be proud to share. This is but a small list of some of the great things that have embodied 2007.

We have stayed in the game and we are winning; and as the fourth quarter comes to a close, we can be extremely encouraged that whatever the year-end score is, it has been made better by the effort of all the company family members. As we look forward into 2008 and beyond, the seeds of opportunity sown in this year will bear wonderful fruit to fuel future successes.

LETTER 12

Quantum Leap Year

I love leap year. It is an opportunity to have one extra day for something great to happen. It is one extra day for something new to be learned. It is one extra day for me to make a difference. It is a freebie.

This leap year is particularly important because it is upon us and at our company we have so many wonderful opportunities that it is staging to be a Quantum Leap Year. In 2007, we sowed the seeds that will allow us to harvest wonderful things in 2008 and beyond.

In 2007, we increased our sales by over $10,000,000 for another record revenue year. We installed and started up our new extrusion plant, the finest in North America.

We attracted new and important customers and developed excellent relationships that will last long into the future. We developed new formulas and commenced work on new brands that are sure to make big news. In addition to many other wonderful accomplishments, we weathered a fairly significant storm due to the industry recall and unprecedented commodity price increase. Most importantly, we learned from having experienced 2007, and we are smarter and better prepared to meet future challenges for having gone through it.

On a personal note, I was thrilled to see our company become healthier in 2007. With over fifty participants in the Reach program we are frankly a more fit company than we were in 2006. With over 80 in the program in 2008 how can we help but move the needle even higher. Healthier employees mean lower medical costs and that is an "extra cherry on top of the protein shake."

In 2008, our Quantum Leap Year, our company looks to increase revenues, continue to improve operational efficiency, expand our portfolio, and make a huge splash in the pet food world. I assure you there will be hurdles; but working together we will *leap* over them and leave the competition wondering in our wake.

Whether you are a youngster or an old guy like me, plan to use this leap year and the extra day we get to do something great, learn something new, help someone in need, or whatever you need to do to make a difference in your life. Remember your family at home and your family here are depending on you to *leap* in 2008.

LETTER 13

Knowing Which Route to Take

Knowing where you are going is important, but understanding and agreeing which route one will take is equally vital to success. Oftentimes choosing the route becomes more debilitating than making the journey.

Not long ago a friend of mine and I were heading to the airport in Pittsburgh. Much debate ensued as we argued over which route to take. Finally, we decided to take Route 60 instead of Route 79. Unfortunately, we debated so long and so passionately that we missed our flight. After a great deal of begging and $75 each we were on our way. Unfortunately, we missed out on three hours of rest and relaxation we had planned when we arrived at our destination, and did not have enough money for those extra beverages we had hoped to enjoy.

After we allowed ourselves to calm down, we realized that both routes had merit. Each was exactly the same number of miles and the traffic of the 79 route on one hand was offset by construction and tolls going the other route. *If I had only known*, I was left thinking; but unfortunately, I was too convinced I was right to allow my friend to get a word in, and he was equally convinced that he was right and had dug in as hard as I had.

This rather trivial fabrication typifies what quite often happens in business. Unfortunately, the pros and cons are often not quite as stark or easily discerned as in the above, but the ramifications of unproductive debate can be much more significant. So many times companies generate a fantastic plan but fail in the executional phase of that plan. Well intended, passionate and dedicated individuals unwittingly become so invested in their position that the end goal becomes cloudy and seemingly unimportant.

Keeping everything in perspective is essential to productive decision making. The old adage *Stop, Look, and Listen* from when we were children crossing the road applied quite well in this case.

1. Stop arguing your position.
2. Look at the options being presented.
3. Listen to others as they explain their rationale.

I would add one additional step, and that would be to *understand*. When we gain an understanding, most times agreement follows quickly.

These keys will work well in all our lives both at work and at home. When we *Stop, Look, Listen, and Understand* great things happen. This year at our company we have opportunities like never before. Working together we will deliver optimal performance and achieve our goals.

LETTER 14

Embracing Differences

America has been called the Great Melting Pot. It is true that we are an amazing amalgamation of varying cultures, races and religions that together claim the status of greatest nation that has ever existed. It is our differences that make us stronger and better.

Think of a country where we all look alike and have the same ideas. Sounds pretty boring to me and a bit scary. One of history's worst evils, Adolf Hitler, had such a dream – a super race. He and his followers set course on a path and followed it all the way to where it ended – history's unmarked grave of discarded lies.

Just as America itself, our company family is a collection of individuals from various cultures, races, and religions formed into the most potent team ever assembled in the Pet Industry. I cannot even imagine our company without all of our family members. As with our country, a big part of what makes us great is our differences and we should embrace them. We all have different experiences and skills that formed together make us stronger than any of us could be alone.

It is important to remember that the differences that make us great also result in the need for tolerance and understanding. What might be an innocent comment to you and your friends could construe a very different meaning to a person who comes from a different culture or a different set of experiences.

I am asking each and every family member to think about the consequences of our words and actions carefully. Consider the feelings of others and what they may perceive from a seemingly innocent comment or action that could be construed as insensitive.

In addition, I would ask each of you to consider the intent of comments or actions that may appear to be offensive. Before you immediately assume that the person meant to inflict harm, ask yourself is this merely an innocent situation. I would urge you to offer a polite explanation as to why you found the comment distasteful, along with requesting that the individual join you in educating more of our family members as to your feelings.

I am confident that when we engage in these two activities, we can overcome a great deal of potential angst and strengthen the team further. There is no place in our company for inappropriate comments or gestures; and I trust you will join me in guiding us as we proceed down our path to excellence. As is always the case, I urge you to report any offensive behavior to your superior, Human Resources, or me.

LETTER 15

75 and Going Strong

As I reflect on our 75th anniversary, what it means, and our next 75 years and beyond, I continue to be amazed by the gravity of the accomplishment. Existing as the oldest pet food company under the same ownership is quite remarkable and our very bright future is exhilarating. But the most amazing story is the commitment of the family members who have brought us this far and who will continue to take us forward.

Two events during July served as a very enlightening reminder to me of the amazing commitment of our family members past and present. While attending our picnic I had the pleasure of meeting many of our retirees who helped forge the platform on which we now operate. I was touched by their continued interest in our business and the closeness I felt when speaking with them.

Just days after our picnic, I had the honor of hosting a lunch attended by seventeen of our more senior tenured family members. While we were visiting, I realized that in the room there was well over 400 years of service to our company. These family members and many others continue to bless us with their talents, day in and out; and their contributions have been vital to our success.

Whether you are on your first day with our company or your 40th year, your contributions and commitment are the building blocks that will take us forward successfully. Our family is an amazing amalgamation of varying talents, skills and capabilities who together create the most potent force in the pet industry past present and future. With a team of this magnitude, how can our future be anything but the brightest?

LETTER 16

Time

How many of us have said "There just isn't enough time in the day." or "I wish I had more time." Time is a cherished commodity. There has been much written about time and time management. I recently googled "time management" and found over 110 million entries.

One thing on which we can all agree: we cannot add hours to the day or days to the weeks or even weeks to the year. (Though some public companies have unsuccessfully tried.) What we can do is make more of the time we have available.

There are a number of ways to make the most of the time we have. The challenge is how to best tackle the assignment. The answer is there is going to be a unique solution for each of us.

For me it starts with *stop doing*. I examine what tasks I can simply eliminate from my day. We all have to make choices and sometimes they are extremely tough ones, but the need for balance must take precedence. In my personal life I have gone to almost 100% online banking. My check is direct deposit, and all of my bills are paid on line. I can accomplish what used to take me three to four hours a week in less than a half hour. It was uncomfortable at first, but now it is second nature for me.

The next step is to determine what I can do simultaneously. How can I make a task that I either have to do or want to do serve two or more purposes? Again, I will turn to my personal life for an example. On Tuesday evenings I love to watch Law and Order, but this takes time away from the gym, which is also important to me. So every Tuesday at 10 p.m. I settle on the floor and tune in to channel 12. When each commercial commences I can perform exercise for the four minute interval. There are four commercial breaks, so after enjoying an hour of entertainment I have completed 15 minutes of exercise. Almost double the *8-minute abs* of infomercial fame.

In both cases above, technology has made possible what was once impossible. As such we must always be on the lookout for what new inventions are available to help us to achieve our goals.

These simplistic examples in my personal life are easy choices for me. At work, the choices can be much more challenging, but once the correct ones are made the rewards can be much more meaningful.

Simply stated, businesses that learn how to manage time effectively are able to accomplish more with less effort, and in a shorter timeline – those businesses are more apt to win. We are the perfectly sized company to become experts in time management and, in turn, have more opportunities come our way.

Take a good look in the mirror and ask yourself, "Is this a nice to have or a need to have?" and "Is there a better way or a new way to accomplish a task?" I think you will be surprised how much faster and further we can go with this approach.

There is a caution, we must do our homework and ensure that vital tasks are not left undone or underdone. The ramifications of failing to properly assess what is mission critical and what is not can have stark ramifications.

Our challenge is to find the right balance that delivers results while minimizing risk. The same is true both in business and our personal lives, but if we wait too long, we will simply run out of time.

LETTER 17

Feeling Fine in 2009

This promises to be an extremely exciting year. Opportunities abound and our company is poised and ready to take full advantage. In order to be able to make the most of every challenge we must be both *smart* and *healthy*.

Smart is the easy part. I believe we have that one covered. Last time I checked you were all well equipped to function in your respective roles at peak performance. While we can always get smarter, smart does not seem to be a problem here in our business. *Healthy* is a bit more of a challenge and an area that companies often fail to properly assess.

Within *Healthy* there are two very distinct aspects. Individual health is key, and I challenge you all to look inward on your personal health and ask yourself a few questions: Am I taking care of myself properly? What can I do to make an improvement to my health in 2009?

If you have not done so, I urge you to participate in our wellness initiative, *Reach* It is a fun way to feel better and get healthier. It's not too late – in fact, it's never too late to start making a positive change in your life. In 2009, we are going to stress healthy lifestyle choices like never before.

The other aspect of *Healthy* is team health. We have all heard stories of the better team that did not win because they did not function well. In 2009, we are going to focus on becoming the healthiest team in the pet category.

Healthy teams start with *Trust*. It sounds simple, but is often very hard to execute. In order to function at optimum performance we must all admit that each of us has strengths and weaknesses and allow individual team members who have specific strengths to take charge in situations when their skill sets can best accomplish the assignment.

Trust becomes more easily gained when we get to know each other better and admit our weaknesses. For instance, if I come toward a piece of equipment with a wrench someone ought to be able to *stop the madness* before I break something.

Finally, once we start to mine trust we can politely and constructively advise team members when we feel they had erred or acted improperly. Don't try this one without real trust as the consequences may not be so positive.

The transformation to *Healthy* does not happen overnight for individuals. In many cases it takes months and sometimes years of hard work and discipline – and once you have achieved your goal you have to work at it on a regular basis. So is the transformation to a *Healthy* team.

We are a good team, but focusing on becoming *Healthy* will transform us into a great team. It is going to take time and hard work, but the dividends will be well worth it.

Every journey starts with one step in the right direction. Let's make our next step count as we follow the path for a *Healthy* lifestyle. The results will amaze you and we will be "Feeling Fine in 2009."

LETTER 18

You Did It

Last May our company embarked on a very important path. The road to *Food Safety Excellence*. In a nutshell, our company was asked to become a pioneer in food safety by becoming the first bakery in the pet industry to become SQF certified. In a meeting during that month, the seemingly unbelievable set of requirements was described in excruciating detail. A deep breath was exhaled and was followed by a commitment – and then we were off on a remarkable and daunting journey.

Since it had never been done before, you really did not know exactly what to expect; but you did know that like all pioneers, the path you would travel would be wrought with twists, turns and unexpected pitfalls. You were not disappointed.

After eleven months, a commitment from every associate, and a great deal of blood sweat and even a few tears, your dream has become a reality. *Excellence in food safety* is our company. Bravo to everyone involved. Your resilience, fortitude, and intensity have paid off.

Now we sit alone at the top of bakeries in the pet category. The position is exhilarating, but has a stark responsibility. Yes, staying

FIRESTARTER

on top can oftentimes be harder than making it there. In the weeks, months and years ahead our company will be challenged to continue to excel in the area of food safety.

LETTER 19

And the Survey Says

I grew up with *The Family Feud*. Every evening Richard Dawson would lead two families into battle with that famous line. I happened across it again almost 40 years later. The hosts have changed but the show remains almost exactly as I remember it as a teenager. Surely it has stood the test of time.

Recently, you all participated in a survey of *likes* and *wish fors* at our company. I want to personally thank each and every one of you for your contribution. The results are in and we are engaged in transforming the data into action. I believe in the weeks and months to come you will see changes, often subtle ones, which are intended to address your feedback. Bottom line, it is a combination of more of what you like, and enhancements to address those wish fors you shared.

The survey is only one type of communication that is available to everyone here to share their views. I urge you to take advantage of every opportunity to share your opinions that you believe will help make our company an even better place to work than it is today. We encourage you to talk with your supervisors and lead people on a regular basis. Additionally, everyone on the Executive Team and Lead Team is available for a chat.

Communication is certainly not a one-way street, but rather a web of information across the organization and beyond to trading partners, consumers, and interested parties. We are committed to continue to share our road map forward with every family member, and I urge you to ask questions and provide feedback if you believe there is a better way to share information or if questions arise.

In addition to the communication already in place, very shortly you will see a suggestion box placed in the lunchroom. If you submit a question and include your name we will get you an answer within a week. If you are more comfortable remaining anonymous, we will address legitimate questions but formal responses will be impossible. The box will be opened every Monday and responses will be returned by the following Monday. It is up to all of us who work here to make this program a success.

Our company has a rich 76-year history and it is our responsibility to ensure that we continue to stand the test of time. Through enriched communication we all learn, and through learning we become smarter and make better decisions. Every sunrise is illuminated with opportunity and each sunset is a time for reflection. Let us make the most of each day that lies ahead.

LETTER 20

Thanksgiving

Each year as the days get shorter and the cold north wind paints the countryside with the beautiful colors that only mother nature creates, I begin to reflect on the year and the blessings that have been bestowed upon me. 2009 has been a true bounty for our family and I wanted to take this opportunity to thank you all for your support, friendship and hard work.

Our country has undergone one of the most challenging periods in its history. Our economy is sluggish, and we are immersed in an increasingly troubling conflict in the Middle East. In Meadville, we have seen our neighbors lose their jobs and struggle to make ends meet.

At our company, we have reaped the bounty that was sown over years of hard work. There is no question – we are having a notable year. Everyone's exceptional efforts and sacrifices that contributed to create this success has not gone unnoticed by me. I do not think I can say *thank you* enough and I am confident that this team has what it takes to take us to the next level and beyond.

I want to offer a special thank you to all of your families who support all of us as we travel this road. Without their love and patience our success would have been most probably impossible and certainly not as rewarding.

I look forward to celebrating this stellar year with all of you at the Christmas party. I hope to see you all there. Until then, I wish you all a very blessed and Happy Thanksgiving. I look forward to working with all of you to create a long and sustained successful future for the entire company family.

LETTER 21

Simply Four

We have completed the work on our 2014 Strategic Plan and I am excited about the direction our company is going. We have seen phenomenal growth and unprecedented success over this past year, and the work we have accomplished and the plans we have completed will serve us well as we head into this next phase of our evolution.

Countless hours and a great deal of effort and energy have been committed to the completion of this road map to the future, and the details are both provocative and insightful. On a broad scale it comes down to four simple themes that we must all rally around:

1. **Great People Doing Extraordinary Things** – We have the best team in the pet industry and as we have grown we continue to develop our competencies. In order to function at our best we must remember that all great teams start and end with trust. An aligned team is a powerful weapon, and this team is capable and ready to tackle the challenges of the future world.

2. **Safe Supply Chain** – Food safety will continue to be our top priority and we must not stumble in this area. We need every company family member to champion food safety, and working together we will excel in this area.

3. **Building Brands That Our Company Owns** – We have developed an effective business model that includes a combination of our brands, retailer brands, and custom manufacturing. While each leg of the stool is vital to our success, we will focus on building our brands. We will start by making sure Plaid and Nutrish are successful. At the same time, two important groups, New Ventures and Innovation, will be developing exciting and compelling branded propositions.

4. **Customer Intimacy** – We will build on our 76-year heritage of world-class customer service, and complement it with insightful analysis and category expertise that will be unparalleled in the industry. Our larger competitors have way too much time and money invested in their paradigms to effectively meet our challenge, and are simply not as fast or nimble as we are.

Keeping these four principles at the top of our minds is the key to future success. , complemented with our pledge that **Every Day You Get Our Very Best,** is a potent platform on which we will build our collective futures.

LETTER 22

Better Together

On February 1, 2010, a new division, headquartered in Dumas, Arkansas, joined our company family. This is a very important event in our company's history and will be vital as we forge our future together. While a great deal of work was completed to bring the deal to reality much is yet to be done to unlock the potential of a bigger juggernaut.

Our company completed this transaction with three major strategic imperatives in mind. Firstly, our quest for additional capacity and an enhanced supply chain took us to a number of regions and communities throughout the United States. The Dumas facility offers a unique opportunity as we can add significant, incremental capacity in a very short period to an industry that is severely under capacity.

Peeling the onion back, we found two other very interesting opportunities unique to the Arkansas division. In their portfolio of brands were a couple of very interesting offerings. While we continue to evaluate all the specifics, it is safe to say that these brands appeal to a very different consumer than our existing family of brands. We believe that there is significant upside potential with these target consumers.

Finally, and most importantly, when we got to know the people from our Arkansas division, we found them to be a very dedicated and passionate team. Their values very closely mirrored our company's core values. It is clear that the Arkansas team members will quickly become key participants in the success of our new enterprise.

Over the next five months we will be completing phase one of the integration. It will consist of four important elements:

1. **Commercial side integration** – This will include learning from the Arkansas sales team and sharing with them our vision and go-to market strategy. Additionally, we will be framing our future direction for the "new" brands.

2. **Operational Excellence** – We will build on the foundation crafted by the Arkansas team to provide best-in-class food safety, people safety, and service.

3. **Plant enhancement project** – A team will be completing a project to bring substantial incremental capacity and capability to the operation.

4. **Synergy Assessment** – we will be examining both the existing organization and the Arkansas organization in a quest for best practices. Once opportunities are identified they will be prioritized and scheduled for completion.

It is sure to be an exciting road to travel. I would request that all our expanded company family members support the integration by doing the following:

1. Remember to take care of your current responsibilities by giving your best every day.

2. Be prepared to offer your ideas and suggestions and do not be afraid to ask questions.

3. Remember to be considerate of others who might be distracted as they attempt to complete the integration work. Offer support as is appropriate.

Please join me in welcoming the Arkansas organization and all of the fantastic people to the company family. I hope you are as excited as I am about the opportunities this brings to our future.

LETTER 23

Managing Change

Change is a word that elicits a spectrum of emotions unlike most others. Change both excites and angers. It can scare and provide comfort. Change is capable of generating hope and creating despair. Sometimes it precipitates a wide variety of feelings all at the same time.

At our company we have been experiencing unprecedented change over the past several years. In 2010, the change seems to have risen to new heights. How we manage the change will be key to optimizing future success. There are a few tried and true rules that are effective in mastering change.

1. Talk about it in a positive light with a trusted friend, family member or supervisor.
2. Ask others to support you through the change.
3. Look into the future and place the change into perspective.
4. Ask yourself if this will really matter in five or ten years.

About 24 years ago I was in a passionate debate with a coworker over a change in corporate policy that required employees to submit copies of their driver's licenses to the company so background checks could be completed. Our new insurance carrier had mandated the requirement. As my coworker's emotions escalated, my patience began to wear thin. Simultaneously, the door burst open and another coworker advised that the space shuttle had just blown up on takeoff. As we raced for the only television set in the office we both realized how trivial the request had been once put into perspective.

As we traverse the changing landscape that embodies the future of our company, I urge you to use the tools above along with others you may have in your tool chest to manage through the change in the most efficient manner. These are indeed extremely exciting times and the change we are experiencing is an essential element of the realization of our team's future goals. I look forward to enjoying many future successes with all of our family members. Long into the future when we reflect back to this period of time in our lives may we well say: "These were amongst the finest times of our careers."

LETTER 24

That's One Small Step

On July 20th 1969, with the entire world watching, The Eagle landed on the moon, and shortly after Neil Armstrong descended the ladder and uttered the now famous line, "That's One Small Step for Man; One Giant Leap for Mankind." The pilot of the Eagle was Buzz Aldrin. Shortly after Armstrong's fateful step, Aldrin joined him on the lunar surface. These two men and the "Eagle" became icons in space exploration history.

Only a few veteran space junkies remember Michael Collins. Michael was the third and arguably the most important member of the crew as he circled the lunar surface piloting the command module, Columbia. Without his skills and dedication the mission would have been unachievable.

As we embark on our mission, one of our four imperatives is *Great People Doing Extraordinary Things*. This starts with attracting and retaining the best individuals and having them take on roles and responsibilities that allow them and the entire team to excel. Each role will have its own unique requirements and family members must be given the latitude to explore new ways to fulfill them.

FIRESTARTER

Some of the responsibilities and roles will place many of our family members in the position to work on new and exciting projects. At the same time, most of us will be ensuring that the core veteran business segments are supported and enriched. Regardless of what assignments our individual and team responsibilities have us tackle, all are equally important. The entire team is counting on each and every family member "giving their best every day"; and when we do, success will be realized and extraordinary things occur.

Our company has the best Collinses, Aldrins, and Armstrongs in the pet category. Together we can and will make history and it starts with "One Small Step."

BOOK 3

Reflections

....

Leadership and learning are
indispensable to each other.

~ John F. Kennedy

Leadership Lessons that Ignite

With the advent of the internet, the opportunity to reach an enormous number of people instantaneously became ordinary. A revolution ensued, as seemingly inconsequential internet posts and videos became pop culture marvels. My favorite item was a fun, yet utterly imbecilic, video created by a man named Psy. His song, titled "Gangnam Style," exploded onto the scene in 2012, and in less than half a year it had exceeded 1 billion views. Fast forward to 2023; that video has been watched over 4.8 billion times.

I was fascinated by this phenomenon and the powerful nature of the new technology. A new term, "going viral," became a household phrase. It was Malcolm Gladwell's timely book, *The Tipping Point*, in action. As an enthusiastic educator, I was drawn to the opportunity that the internet presented.

In 2013 and 2014, I was an active writer of a blog, called Reflections. Two driving forces led to this activity. I had written a book entitled *Unbundle It: Simplify Your Perspective to Live a Better Life and Release the Power of Your Team*. Reflections became part of a multifaceted marketing campaign I employed to help launch a consulting business.

More importantly, I saw the activity as a way to facilitate my transition from a full-time working professional into whatever was to be next.

Each of us values the varying elements of our life differently. For many, a job is merely a means to an end. But for me, work had been intertwined with my life journey and hard-coded into my psyche. It drove me and I feasted off the euphoria that was created by the successes. Oddly, even the failures fueled my passion. So, in a strange twist, I mired myself in the challenges; I delighted in leading teams in leaping hurdles that they themselves felt were unbreachable.

As my children advanced into adulthood, the other driving responsibility of my life was changing. I marveled as each traversed their life's paths, making their own choices.

At that point in my life, I was searching for mental fulfillment, which in my world meant fulfilling God's purpose for me in my remaining time. Among our great blessings is our **earthly tent** – and I believe that nourishing it through a healthy combination of diet and exercise is pleasing to God. For me, contemplating and executing both **mental** and **physical** diligence are symbiotic. Each requires the other to thrive.

As my consulting business grew, I filled my figurative bucket with stimulation and purpose. Reflections ended as it had begun, rather unceremoniously. Interestingly, it was years later that I learned, quite by accident, that at least one follower of my Reflections had been so inspired that he had drafted an article about it. I do not know him, and we will likely never meet, but I began to appreciate the reach and breadth of social media.

It is my hope you will find wisdom and guidance in each Reflection that follows.

A note to the reader: The Reflections are reprinted here as they originally appeared, with the removal of gratuitous marketing blurbs.

REFLECTION 1

Wisdom from a Great Leader

March Madness is behind us and we are heading toward crowning yet another national champion. America loves the tournament as we witness first-hand the passion and discipline of these young athletes transformed by great coaches into potent teams.

The previously relatively unknown team who becomes a fan favorite is among my most enjoyable parts of the tournament. There is really nothing quite like it in sports.

Every March I am reminded that John Wooden, who passed away in 2010, led the UCLA Bruins to ten national championships in twelve years. Arguably the greatest coach ever to lead any team in any sport.

More important than his success on the court were his phenomenal leadership skills and his uniquely humble persona. I believe that John Wooden's true legacy will be the inspiration we can draw from his success and writings.

What follows are a few of my favorite Wooden quotes. I urge you to learn about Wooden's Pyramid of Success as it is a great piece of work to help us in business and in life. I hope you gain some inspiration from the following:

Wooden Quotes

Winning takes talent, to repeat takes character

Things turn out best for the people
who make the best of the way things turn out.

Talent is God given. Be humble. Fame is man-given. Be grateful.
Conceit is self-given. Be careful.

Success is never final, failure is never fatal.
It's courage that counts.

Do not let what you cannot do interfere with what you can do.

Be prepared and be honest.

If you're not making mistakes, then you're not doing anything.
I'm positive that a doer makes mistakes.

Never mistake activity for achievement

Be quick, but don't hurry

Never make excuses. Your friends don't need them
and your foes won't believe them

Listen if you want to be heard

Tell the truth. That way you don't have to remember a story

Until Next Time

REFLECTION 2

The Extra Degree

At 211 degrees water is extremely hot. At 212 degrees it boils and turns to steam. Steam can move a turbine and generate electricity. Certainly, we can all identify with the 'power' of electricity. Without that extra degree we only have hot water and with that single degree the opportunities are vast and far reaching.

The energy required to take water from 211 to 212 degrees is the same amount that it took to elevate the temperature of that same water each of the degrees on its way to this point, but the transformation only occurs when we go this extra degree.

With water the answer is fairly straightforward. We know that the water will boil and turn to steam and we know when that transformation will occur. With other 'unknown' situations we oftentimes can not recognize how close we are to reaching our goal and furthermore the benefits realized from achieving this goal are often misunderstood.

How many times in our lives have we failed to go the extra degree and have failed to achieve our goals? Could it be that we had been so close that an extra 'degree' of effort would have resulted in realization beyond expectations? If so, would that not be a tragedy?

FIRESTARTER

At work and at life when we give the extra degree, great things can and will happen. When a team is functioning well, the group synergy is extremely powerful and success follows. The best functioning team requires every member to go the extra degree. Does your team understand and embrace this concept?

REFLECTION 3

Resolve to Be the Best

We have just entered the second quarter of 2013, and most New Year's resolutions are already a distant memory. How are you doing with yours? If you are hanging in there, great and keep up the good work; but you are definitely in the minority.

It's not too late to start over, instead of making a bunch of well intentioned but probably unachievable promises that despite your "best" efforts you fail to keep and then "fall off the wagon" and wait for the calendar to turn another year to try again, let's resolve to be the best we can be. We can start today.

The best part is we do not need to wait for the calendar to decide to make a change in our lives. One of my favorite sayings is "I can't do anything about what happened in the past but to learn from it" – and so let's resolve to learn from past mistakes or "bad luck" and commit to do everything in our power to make the future better. If you stumble, determine what you can learn from the *fall* and start again – smarter and better equipped to succeed.

Frankly, each of us should have a long term plan for our life journey. It should be succinct, visible, and stretching but achievable. For those who have not tackled life goal setting the exercise might appear to be daunting. Since they are your goals the task of developing them can be one of the most liberating and cathartic exercises ever.

Our life journey is the most important expedition we will encounter, yet many fail to have the road map on where they want to go or the road they desire to travel to get there. If it feels a bit overwhelming then start with a few short term transactional goals that are easily achievable. Once you have tackled these mini goals the success will energize you to move forward. Nothing builds confidence more than success.

It might be most effective to have a good friend or loved one help you stay on track. Choose wisely, these accountability partners need to introduce *tough love* when it is warranted.

Applying the attitude that *I can change what I desire to change* is extremely powerful. At home, at work, and at play, resolving to be the best will pay huge dividends. Do not wait for next year or even next week. Start today.

REFLECTION 4

Differentiation

Anyone who watched the NFL draft over the past week witnessed differentiation in action. Each team evaluated the talent pool available at the time of their selection. They evaluated the team's need, style of play, team's values and other important factors prior to making their selection.

I did not hear any outcry on how cruel and unfair this process is to the draftees. Quite the contrary, the process is met with an unbelievable amount of excitement and anticipation.

Provided it is executed properly, applying differentiation to business will deliver remarkable results. Yet, I constantly hear how unfair and risky the process is. Actually, when handled properly it is liberating, powerful, and energizing.

"But someone has to be last and that is not fair."

Nothing could be further from the truth. Those individuals who are viewed by the company as the worst performers normally fall into one of three categories.

1. Poor performers who drag the team down and should be exited from the business.
2. Good people who have lost their way or are struggling. The exercise of differentiation normally provides a needed "wake

up call" and their performance escalates.

3. Good people in the wrong job. A reassignment to a position that better suits their skill set regularly pays significant dividends.

In all cases the company wins and in most cases the employee wins as well. In my experience those individuals in any of the three categories listed are unhappy and even those who exited the company employ end up in a better place as they ultimately find work where they can become productive members of the team.

I have not addressed the top performer and the fully effective performer status in this missive, but through the process of differentiation the remainder of the team will fall into categories and there are specific actions required by the company to fuel these folks to their highest potential.

The NFL calls the final person picked in the draft as Mr. Irrelevant. This year it is Justice Cunningham. I am sure he is a happy man today. While being the last player picked in the draft is far different from the bottom person on a differentiation grid, the fact remains: in life and in business – someone is first, someone is last, and everyone else falls in between.

REFLECTION 5

Personality Typing – An Investment for Success

I have come to believe that there is always something new to learn about ourselves and our coworkers. As is most often the case, the more educated we become the more adept we are at realizing optimal outcomes of any of a variety of experiences.

Have you ever wondered why some individuals simply seem to be at odds with others? In many cases it might simply be one individual's predisposition on how to react to a certain opportunity. For example, it is always my first inclination to immediately immerse myself into an opportunity and attempt to find an expedited solution. A coworker might take the approach to think about the broader implications and take no action until he or she frames the broader repercussions.

I am left to wonder why my coworker is making it so difficult and thus wasting time and money. My coworker cringes at my seemingly reckless behavior and sees me as irresponsible. Uneducated, we start to sow the seeds of an unhealthy relationship. When we understand each other's personality preferences we can predict how each of our team members will act under differing scenarios.

In order to help optimize team performance, an investment in personality typing is an essential tool. I find the Myers Briggs approach to be an excellent resource.

The Myers Briggs approach theorizes that there are 16 different personality types. It is important to note that none of these personality types is superior to another and in fact it is preferred that teams incorporate a blend of personality types.

Once we understand our preferences we can better identify where potential pain points can reside. Equally important, when we know the personality preferences of our coworkers we can better understand drivers for their conduct.

Imagine how powerful it would be to have an amalgamation of personality types working together productively to drive your organization to the next level. When we embrace our differences and have the permission to engage in candid discussions over the pros and cons of vying approaches, we give ourselves the best opportunity for sustained success.

REFLECTION 6

Unions

During my travels, the number one challenge I receive from company leaders who have unionized workforces is the chronic issue of exiting an individual. I regularly hear that Union rules preclude the adoption of the principles I teach.

I have worked with unionized workforces for much of my career. Admittedly, the introduction of unionized workforces adds a level of complexity; but to suggest that this precludes a company from successfully implementing this productive program is nonsense. In fact, in many cases a properly managed union relationship makes it much easier to implement such programs. The problem comes from weak management who has unwittingly empowered the union and in doing so created an untenable situation that makes it quite difficult to successfully implement almost anything but the basic transactional day to day requirements.

Unions live and prosper through these basic principles:

1. The Contract – the terms and conditions under which the parties must act.
2. Seniority – the tenure of the individuals who are covered by the contract.

3. Past Practice – any of a variety of acts the management has allowed in the past.

In my experience contracts are rarely an impediment to productive work environments. The challenge normally is that management is not trained on the content of the contract. Contracts are regularly held up by union operatives as overarching guides that restrict management's ability to implement change. While it is possible that restrictive language can be included into contract codicils, I have found more often than not no such language exists, or the language has been misinterpreted by union operatives to their benefit.

I have yet to work with a company where line management had a keen understanding of the contract language and its implications. On the flip side, union stewards are almost always well-educated on them and in fact regularly have a copy in their pocket. In fact, often members of management think that the union contracts are unwieldy and complicated and as such not capable of being easily understood.

Seniority is easy. Have a seniority list available and do not deviate from it. The real challenges come from the addition of past practice. Normally, weak or uneducated managers allow union members to bend or break the rules and in doing so create a whole list of past practices that create chaos for management in the future.

The trick is to have the courage to never allow any deviation from the rules currently in place. Union environments are black and white and there is no gray. Once a "favor" is allowed by a member of management, the union quickly cites past practice and another work rule moves from management control to union regulation.

Refusal to agree to seemingly innocent requests or "favors" is one of the hardest management challenges. At times the refusal to allow favors feels cruel. I would advise managers to cite union rules and add that "my hands are tied." Over time, I have found that union members, faced with such realities, urge their leaders to make regulations more management friendly. One thing union leaders normally have in common with management is the desire to keep their lives as hassle free as possible and as such will work with management to find a solution once the rank and file pressures them to do so.

As it pertains to the exit of unionized employees this can be accomplished if management is willing to perform the due diligence to successfully build the case for termination. Most often, management is either uneducated or unwilling to meet this standard. To predispose that it is impossible or almost impossible to exit unionized employees is simply an excuse that management uses to validate the false realities of their plight.

REFLECTION 7

Eight Point Plan for a Powerful Team

As part of the series on healthy team tips I reflected on all I have read and all I have written on the subject. I think it distills down to a fairly straightforward set of imperatives.

If you want a highly functioning team, it is as simple as this eight point guideline:

1. Engage a group that shares your core values.
2. Set aspirational yet achievable goals for the company and every individual.
3. Create an environment that encourages and rewards trust.
4. Empower every individual to create and achieve greatness.
5. Persuade them to stretch.
6. Love them when they fail.
7. Create an environment that encourages and rewards self-discipline.
8. Have the courage to exit those from the team who do not fit.

I believe that the final point may be the most difficult one by which to live. Most of us shirk at the thought of having an uncomfortable conversation. The fact is they are not fun, but very necessary. In my experience the agony over thinking about them usually eclipses the actual conversation. Simply stated, we need to transform the agony and worry into action for the good of the broader team.

REFLECTION 8

When 50 Percent is More Than 100 Percent

I want it all. It's a fairly common sentiment in business. Normally, getting it all is extremely beneficial. Frequently, businesses are incapable of achieving the desired outcome without help or support. Business leaders are quick to consider options available to them to assist the company in achieving the goal. This often includes hiring consulting firms or advisors all who come with a hefty price tag.

A business owns a brand that is struggling and is faced with a dilemma. Do we throw more money at it? Do we cut our losses? Do we sell the brand? Is it worth anything?

The previous questions come into play and retained advisors provide their input. A decision is made to kill or sell the brand and the company moves on to the next hurdle.

One important question is frequently left unasked. Is there some entity that has the capability to help make the brand successful who might be interested in sharing the brand with my organization?

I have found that far too often, companies kill brands and allow them to languish in the bottom of a filing cabinet or worse yet sell the brand at a below market value creating a new competitor. I recommend that careful consideration be given to collaborating with a new partner who is willing to share the risk in exchange for some equity.

As I see it, there is little downside. Provided you have properly vetted your new partner, there is tremendous potential to create wealth using this approach. Further, you have just added a passionate advocate for the brand who is predisposed to make it successful. Even better, this resource is not part of your normal team and thus does not create a material drain on the organization's capacity.

If orchestrated properly, it costs the original owner nothing other than a portion of the potential profits. This has led me to come to the conclusion that 50 percent of a big number is more than 100 percent of a small one.

Is it time for you to consider this approach?

REFLECTION 9

The Art of Rationalization – The Hidden Enemy

We all do it. It might be as simple as having another piece of pie and then promising yourself that you will exercise to work it off. We rationalize that it is acceptable to do something or not do something because of some reason that is oftentimes totally unrelated or completely false.

In fact the word Rationalize is defined as:

Attempt to explain or justify (one's own or another's behavior or attitude) with logical, plausible reasons, even if these are not true...

In business, it takes on a life of its own and can have dire consequences. A quality test takes too long to perform and an employee has a date that night. "That test never comes back bad anyway," the employee rationalizes. The paperwork is fudged or better known as *pencil whipped* and the company is left vulnerable.

Employees rationalize that they are underpaid or not appreciated and they commence exhibiting substandard behavior. This can lead to falsifying time cards, stealing, or violating company policy. "The company won't miss this and besides they are making a bunch of money anyhow," is a common statement.

Leaders rationalize as well. They may decide that it's ok for employees to work in less than desirable working conditions or work exhausting hours. "They are getting paid overtime so it's not my problem."

Eventually, rationalization if left unchecked leads to entitlement. Entitlement leads to complacency and laziness or expectations that are not founded in prudence. As the entitlement specter invades your organization productivity is negatively impacted, organizational capacity erodes, and the cost of doing business increases.

I recall a junior employee securing a premium rental car equipped with the GPS package for a rental that required him to drive less than 20 miles. Upon questioning, he revealed that his superior had directed him never to rent anything less than a premium car because "that's the way we do it here." The 2-day rental was over $300 or $15 a mile. His entitled boss had come to believe that he and his team deserved such treatment. Likely he has an expectation and believes that he might lose his "deserved" status if others do not join along.

This example is a fairly benign one; but it illustrates the broader point of entitlement leading to increased costs. It is vitally important that as business leaders we are constantly on the lookout for rationalizers in our midst – as well as our own predisposition to rationalize.

REFLECTION 10

Managing Emotionally Charged Situations

I think it is fair to say that most of us have experienced a situation where we have had to manage through emotional outbursts from time to time. In some cases it might even be a situation that we ourselves incited.

There are a number of tools that we can use to help prevent these situations from occurring. These would run the gamut of adopting and following a clear and concise communication plan through purposeful training of all team members on skills to manage emotions in the workplace.

As leaders, it is our responsibility to educate ourselves on how to manage these situations and it starts with us "checking our emotions at the door" before we act or react to an emotionally charged situation.

Individuals normally become emotional when they are afraid. Fear drives most negative behavior. Underlying drivers for fear in the workplace include fear of losing something, fear of not fitting in, fear of embarrassment, fear of inferiority, and fear of losing a self-perceived image that one might have for themselves.

At the apex of an emotional outburst fear drives irrational behavior and at times it can become a threat to the safety of your team members. Normally, it does not transcend to this level but regularly there are elevated voices or yelling. People normally yell because they do not think they are being heard.

In the midst of an episode our first responsibility is to get the emotion out of the situation. This can be done by unemotionally asking questions of the perpetrator. This is often described as bringing people down their emotional ladder. The reference probably derives from the Ladder of Inference that states that individuals start with one set of facts and interpret them often improperly, and ultimately take action based on a misconception. There are plenty of good references available on this reality.

Removing the emotion from the conversation can be as simple as asking a few questions and urging the other party to help you understand the source of their frustration. This is known as active listening. Active listening can be used in three areas – information – affirmation – inflammation.

Information's goal is to get a clear picture of what is going on. This requires us to ask questions, restate what you heard so there is no confusion, and finally to summarize what you heard.

Affirmation is used when we want to explore the problem. Clearly identify the problem or situation and then try to understand why this situation is resulting in the emotion. Questions like what is it about this situation that makes you feel the way you do. We should acknowledge that the individual's feelings are understandable while we probe deeper. In most cases, individuals feel validated once they have been heard and you have demonstrated you have listened and "heard."

Inflammation is responding to an attack on you. It is understandable for your first response to be to defend yourself. This normally only inflames the situation further.

Our first step should be to get the emotion out of the conversation. Normally once a person knows you are listening to them the emotion quickly subsides. Comments such as "I see this is extremely upsetting to you, help me understand it" can help reduce the emotion. We should be ready to acknowledge their side and be open to changing our approach when we can, to reduce tension in the future.

These are relatively easy skills to learn but it takes commitment and that commitment must start at the top of the organization. Give it a try and see what happens.

REFLECTION 11

Embracing Cultural Differences

The Globalization of business is a reality. If we are going to compete and win in the global economy we must be prepared to understand and embrace cultural differences. The first thing we need to understand is that the term common sense is an oxymoron. In the global economy there is nothing that is known commonly.

When we commence our education on examining cultural differences we must look beyond the obvious. Language, skin color, and attire are visible differences, but the more important ones are unseen such as beliefs, values, perceptions, and attitudes. Unintended consequences from failure to understand these differences can be debilitating.

For example, cultures tend to be either monochronic or polychronic. A monochronic culture tends to want to do one thing at a time and a polychronic culture will do many things at once. Imagine how offended a person from a monochronic culture like Germany might become when an American is constantly interrupting.

The same is true for cultural orientation differences. A person from a past oriented culture like China might be offended by an

American with a future orientation when he or she fails to recognize the importance of following the proper protocol. Conversely an American might become frustrated by what they deem a waste of time from having to follow some misunderstood and seemingly esoteric etiquette.

Quantity of time is another important cultural difference. In Latin America time is not valued in the same way as it is in the United States. As such, meetings often start late, and team members from the United States become frustrated and often view their counterparts as lazy. On the flip side those counterparts see business people from the United States as being overly preoccupied with work to the point that it becomes a detriment.

There are several other cultural imperatives that must be understood and embraced for optimum relations to be realized. Even things as simple as hand gestures and colors can incite unintended adverse response.

In many eastern cultures red is used in weddings and white is associated with death. The OK hand sign is offensive in Brazil, in Russia it stands for zero, and in Japan it means money.

Education is the key to preparing your team for optimized global interaction. Proper education can help your team become culture-embracing juggernauts.

REFLECTION 12

Back To School Class #1: Red Light - Yellow Light - Green Light

When September arrives and the air temperatures start to cool, two things immediately come to mind. First, I must prepare myself for my annual pilgrimage to my winter home in Florida. More importantly, I am reminded that school is back in session and I am immediately taken back to my youth.

Over the years, I have come to appreciate that many of the games I played and the principles I learned as a child have become the most effective tools to create simplicity in our business lives. I am dedicating the next several Reflections to some of these principles.

Red Light, Yellow Light, Green Light was one of my favorite summer games. Applying the idea of color to just about everything in business and training your team to react to each color, when they see it, is extremely powerful. It allows team members to focus on the areas of concern and prioritize their time accordingly.

Red lights mean high alert and that the task illuminated as such is at high risk for failure – without attention it will not be completed successfully. Yellow lights are warning lights. The item or task highlighted in yellow is behind and could become a problem if not given the proper attention. Items in green status are in line and considered on track for success. As such, less attention is required.

The use of this illumination system can become an extremely effective team enabler. Applying the rule that one team member, if in his or her judgment, feels a project or item is slipping they have the power to move it from Green status to Yellow or Red and from Yellow to Red creates a sense of empowerment.

Conversely, it takes the entire team jointly to approve movement of tasks or projects to Green status. This creates accountability and team unity while avoiding the ability of less capable team members to hide behind "green lights" until it is too late for action.

When the team is in problem solving mode the red lights are easy symbols directing the team member where to focus his or her attention. On the flip side, if a team member is planning on addressing stakeholders on the success of the enterprise the green lights guide him or her to those "winners" that will delight the crowd.

Assigning this color scheme is effective for everything from project management to brands, customers and employees.

REFLECTION 13

Back To School Class #2: Rule of A, B, C

The transitive property in mathematics states that if A = B and B = C then A = C. Applying this simplest of mathematical rules to business dramatically enhances our ability to eliminate mistakes. Simply stated, speed matters in business and if you are constantly looking over your shoulder to correct errors you cannot perform at top speed.

This rule works well to determine if there are errors in reports or analyses. It also is extremely helpful when tracking units or conducting project management. One area where it is particularly helpful is in accounting for inventories.

Inventory errors are extremely costly and can be unbelievably time consuming to correct. When we scan an inventory listing the first things we can look for are obvious errors. Negative numbers are impossible because there cannot be less than zero of an ingredient, finished goods, or other tangible inventory item. Next, look for inflated or deflated numbers. For example every vessel holds a finite amount. When the inventory exceeds the vessel capacity the number must be in error. Further, when the vessel is half full the inventory should be about half of the vessel's capacity. Vessels can be bins, warehouses, or shelves. If a shelf holds ten books there cannot be eleven on it.

Readers, I can hear you saying, "So what! That's too easy." Watch for these types of simple examples in your workplace either with inventory or any other measurable item. I'll bet that unless you are focusing on this skill set, there are obvious problems "screaming" at you from reports that you never see. Normally, the drivers for this are captured within "the numbers," but are buried within the complexity of the report itself – and no one has been trained to look for them.

Machines rarely make mistakes, but people are a regular source of errors. It's not that these people are particularly haphazard or ineffective but rather because they are bundled up in a world of complexity, unproductive precision, cut and paste errors, and beauty pageant reporting.

For those unfamiliar with the term beauty pageant reporting it is none other than the process of making reports look nice to satiate the misguided perception that reports going to executives must look *good*. It is true that executives prefer to have coherent reporting that reads easily, but appearance should never trump accuracy. The same is true for precision. A precise report that is inaccurate is worthless. Find me a boss that prefers a *pretty report* over an accurate one and I'll advise you to start exploring the job market.

REFLECTION 14

Back To School Class #3: The Rule of Too Much Water

When teams are overworked or not functioning at a high level, they tend to spiral out of control, or at a minimum, spiral to a place of great stress. Normally, the gut reaction is to throw more people at the problem. In some cases additional resources are warranted. In others, the current lack of disciplined conduct drives inefficient behavior making it appear that additional resources are needed.

When additional resources are warranted, the question becomes what amount of incremental resources is required? Tragically, those waist-deep in the environment will almost always overcall the number of resources required. This overcall is a result of the uncontrolled situation that is paramount in their minds. In many cases, they do not overcall the resource requirement intentionally; rather, they fervently believe the resources requested are required.

I came up with a demonstration that almost always gets the point across and often gets folks literally jumping out of their seats. I call this exercise *Too Much Water*. I simply get three empty glasses and a large picture of water. I start by filling one glass to a controllable amount. I describe the glass as a resource, and the water is the work. Individuals in the room normally nod their heads in alignment with the exercise. Next, I overfill the second glass until it starts to run onto the table. I continue to pour until what appears to be an insurmountable amount of water is running across the table.

The team and I will usually agree that when there is too much work for the available resources it feels like the uncontrolled running of the water across the table. Next, I take a paper towel or two and mop up the water and squeeze it into the third glass which usually only fills one fourth of the way full. From time to time, I hear complaints that some of the water has fallen on the floor. I usually offer to repeat the exercise by proposing to dump the first glass of water onto the table to determine if the team feels like what was originally spilled was more or less than the contents of the full glass. I have yet to get any takers.

Once the team believes that the under-resource situation is not as severe as it might appear, much better decisions can be made about the level of resource required to resolve the dilemma. If you prefer not to use water, marbles make a good substitute.

Over-resourcing creates its own host of challenges. Whether it is too much water or too many glasses neither is optimal. Identifying how much "water" and how many "glasses" are required to successfully manage the "waterflow" is key. Notching it up to the next level, discovering what "water" is "polluted" and which "glasses" are "ineffective" propels the business beyond the competitive set.

REFLECTION 15

Back To School Class #4: The Tsunami Factor

Prior to the catastrophic events in Indonesia in 2004, Tsunami was not an everyday word. It has become part of our lexicon due to the recent natural disasters created by these tidal waves. In 1995, I coined the term The Tsunami Factor to describe how corporate headquarters' decisions oftentimes adversely affect the field operations. Failure to understand implications of decisions can play havoc with those required to successfully execute the deliverables.

To understand The Tsunami Factor we need to review a bit about the tsunami. A tsunami is created when the ocean floor shifts due to an earthquake. When the earth shifts vertically, the force generated starts a swell in the ocean. The swell might appear to be just another wave out in the depths of the ocean, but it is carrying significant force.

Since the spot where the earthquake might take place is several miles deep, there is a vast area of water to absorb the energy. As the ocean floor rises toward land, the energy is concentrated in a much smaller area. As the wave approaches land, it crests, releasing the energy and causing devastation.

FIRESTARTER

As the story is told, many times Japanese fishermen would be out at sea and return home only to find their villages completely destroyed, never themselves feeling the tsunami that may have passed beneath them earlier in the day.

The same is true with some decisions made at the corporate level. They sound like fairly innocuous directives, but when they make their way to the field, the impact creates devastating results.

A good trusting relationship with fluid, candid and two-way communication between the corporate office and field operations can help ensure the self-created tsunamis are avoided. Notching up trust, instilling candor, and educating the team on how to effectively communicate genuine risks and the realities of the limitations of each business unit is key. Making this a core competency will ensure smooth waters ahead.

REFLECTION 16

Back To School Class #5: Rule of Fishing

I have spent a lifetime fishing. Over the decades I have learned a few essential tips that make me a better fisherman. My target is to enrich my experience by catching not the most fish but the best fish. Those ones I can regale about over and over again.

Building the right team is very similar to fishing. I like to refer to it as *fishing for teammates*. Applying some of the principles that had made me a more accomplished angler can be applied to searching for team members.

1. **Know The Target Fish** – Prior to a search we should understand exactly what type of person we seek to join the team. What does the perfect candidate look like? What skills, knowledge, acumen, and experience are we seeking? Most importantly what values do we want this person to have or in other words will this person "fit" in our company.

2. **The Right Equipment and Baits are required to Catch the Target Fish** – Have we examined the demographics and the competitive landscape? Do we know what combination

of salary, benefits, and associated perks will be required to attract the talent we seek?

3. **Fish Where the Fish Are** – We wouldn't consider fishing in a lake when our target species live in the ocean, but regularly we look in the wrong places for prospects to join our team. Have we determined where we should look to have the best chance of finding the perfect candidate? For example every year high schools across the country graduate a significant number of students who do not plan to go to college. Rarely have I ever seen local business partners with high schools to attract the best and brightest to fulfill entry level jobs.

4. **The First to the Hungry Fish Catches the Best Fish** – Speed matters in fishing (that's why the motors are so big on fishing boats) and speed matters when seeking talent. Have you considered how to be the first to find the target candidates you seek? In each pool of candidates there are only a few top prospects. Once a candidate has accepted a position the likelihood that they will even consider an interview is very low. Frankly, a prospect that has committed to a job and continues to interview is more than likely a person you do not want as part of your team.

5. **A Great Guide Can Be Irreplaceable** – Many business people either don't have the time, resources, or the expertise to become world class at attracting the right talent. Partnering with someone who is a world class employee search professional often is an essential element in successfully building the best team.

Fishing for employees can be as much fun as recreational fishing and much more rewarding. When we catch our recreational fish we

Book 3 Reflections

take a picture and release it back into the water or we take it home and feast for an evening. And we have stories that will last a lifetime.

When we catch that perfect team member we invest in training and recognition and we feast for a lifetime. And we create wealth that will fund recreational fishing trips for a lifetime.

REFLECTION 17

Back To School Class #6:
Four Square

When I was a young lad four square was a game we played at recess. In fact the familiar grid was a regular and permanent site at playgrounds across the country.

In business the four-square grid is amongst the most effective tools for evaluating competing items. These items can be everything from customers, to projects, to people.

A four-square grid will have two axes. On each axis will be one aspect for evaluation. For example, for a customer one axis might be size or scale and the other might be growth potential.

Each quadrant will have a unique descriptor. In the above example we would have Large and Growing, Small and Growing, Large and Declining, and Small and Declining. The team will decide how to approach customers that fall into each quadrant. For example, Large and Growing might be a top priority and investment dollars will be allocated for these accounts. Similarly Small and Growing would be handled in a comparable fashion but on a scale that the account metrics could absorb.

The Small and Declining quadrant should be fairly straightforward. The team could decide to disengage with these accounts or put them on life support. Large and Declining might be the toughest customer set to evaluate. Many on the team will be tempted to give these accounts more attention than they deserve. It will be a team call on how to handle this set, but the indicated actions would suggest we keep these accounts serviced but reduce investment. The team might classify these accounts as transactional. In any case they should be the highest margin accounts in the portfolio and the extra margin generated should be invested against the accounts in the growing category.

With each quadrant the accounts will be force-ranked. This is important during times when funds are not as readily available as other times so we know what action to take within a specific quadrant.

The four-square grid is extremely effective when making decisions on projects and related activities. In these cases, we might use effort and impact as the labels on each axis. Customers, people, projects, and skus all can be evaluated efficiently and effectively using the four-square grid.

REFLECTION 18

Back To School Class #7: Archery Class

When I attended college at the prestigious Slippery Rock State College an archery class was offered as part of the curriculum. Quickly, participants learned that "hitting the bull's-eye" was the desired outcome each and every time an arrow was nocked and the string was drawn back. Sights helped with accuracy and precision. When a sight was bumped even the most precise archers would fail to achieve the goal as their extremely specific pattern was rendered not accurate.

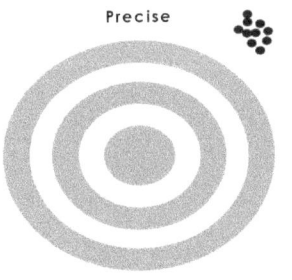

The same is true in business. In a world based in analytics, many pride themselves in delivering extremely detailed and precise worksheets. Two potential negative outcomes are regularly generated by this tedious activity. Firstly, and most importantly, the quest for precision has an adverse impact on accuracy and the data is rendered worthless.

Secondly, the time required to prepare, print and review these monolithic creations reduced the organization's capacity. As such, many important tasks remain uncompleted, and many opportunities are left unexplored.

It's important that we balance accuracy and precision as appropriate for the task at hand. My experience is that most tend to allow precision to be overemphasized and accuracy unintendedly suffers. As such, never allow precision to trump accuracy.

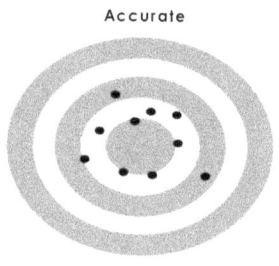

Whether you are a lifelong archer or never drew a nocked arrow, learning this technique will be instrumental in helping your organization hit the target every time. All joking aside, I received an excellent education at SRSC and would not trade the experience for any other.

REFLECTION 19

Back To School Class #8: Dig until You Can No Longer Dig

We often hear, "We just need to dig our way out of this problem." I agree that there are times when you simply need to fight through an issue. Far too often we just keep digging and digging and digging. The digging makes us feel good because we are throwing resources against the problem.

The question should be, why are we digging and how will the digging solve the problem? The reality is, we chose to dig our way out of the problem having no idea what caused the dilemma. I offer the following approach as an alternative. Identify the root drivers of the problem and then determine if digging is even required.

In the most extreme cases you employ a digger while you perform the evaluation. The digger might be digging in vain; but once we understand the drivers, we can apply the appropriate response. One response might be to dig while we solve the dilemma.

One of the classic examples is the job of reconciliation. Over the years I have seen teams of people whose sole job is to reconcile differences between two sets of numbers. Their goal is to make sure both sets of numbers are the same. As they find differences, they dig in to understand what created the disparity.

Once the culprit is discovered, the error is corrected. The reconciler moves on to the next discrepancy. This process is repeated day after day and month after month. It has always amazed me that these people never attempted to change the behavior that created the situation.

Tragically, these types of jobs exist in businesses around the world. Senior management is unaware of the dysfunction on a regular basis. I would challenge leaders to unbundle this type of activity. Put down the shovels, and seek to understand drivers that create the need for diggers and find ways to remedy them.

REFLECTION 20

A Coach – Why?

I was at an event over the weekend and a friend who I had not seen for a while poked me about my change in my Linked In profile that declared me as a coach. "What's that all about?" he joked.

My answer was quick, "Ask the Kansas City Chiefs!" Through week seven the Kansas City Chiefs are the only unbeaten team in football. Prior to the beginning of the season I do not believe that many, if any but the most ardent Chief fans, would have predicted that they would open the season with a perfect 7-0 record. Further, the prediction that the Chiefs would stand as the only unbeaten NFL team after week seven would have been considered a folly.

For those unfamiliar with the NFL, The Kansas City Chiefs posted a disappointing 2-14 record last year. This proud team and its supportive fan base have suffered in recent years with underperformance and an almost *revolving door* of staff changes.

So what changed that enabled this former juggernaut to return to its highly competitive state? In a nutshell, most would credit the addition of Andy Reid as the head coach. To be fair, there have been some personnel changes, but most would agree that Andy Reid has been the keystone of success.

In business, oftentimes we fail to adequately understand the importance of a coach. Business and life coaches are important elements in the development of an enterprise or an individual. When selecting a coach the most important element is fit. Does this person fit the values of the enterprise or individual? Once fit is established trust can follow, and when there is trust coaches can be game changers.

Two distinct areas where coaches can play a unique role are perspective and candor. Coaches, since they did not grow up in the organization, will come with a very unique perspective. Equally importantly, a good coach will tell you what you do not want to hear: Candor. He or she will quickly become your organization's *canary in the cage,* and assuming that role can help the organization, avoid the disastrous consequences of unintended actions.

A good coach is worth his or her weight in gold. Just ask the Kansas City Chiefs and their fan base. Arrowhead stadium, the home of the Kansas City Chiefs is the most amazing venue in the NFL. The stadium design and the rabid fan base broke the Guinness Book of World Records for recording the highest noise level in an outdoor stadium on October 13 of this year.

I've had the pleasure of visiting Arrowhead in the good times and the bad. The loyal fan base supports the team through all times, but the passion and energy created when the team is winning is *World Record Breaking*. The power is awe inspiring.

REFLECTION 21

Giving Thanks

Each year as the days get shorter and the cold north wind paints the countryside with the beautiful colors that only Mother Nature creates, I begin to reflect on the year and the blessings that have been bestowed upon me. Candidly, since I relocated to Florida a few years ago I find myself missing the experience. All but for a few short business trips, fall's beauty lives only in my memory.

2013 has been a true bounty for me and I wanted to take this opportunity to thank you all for your support, friendship and well wishes. With this emotional backing I have had the blessing of realizing some of my dreams. A marriage this past spring and the opportunity to teach at our local college this past summer stand tall in my memory.

As Thanksgiving passes we head into the holiday season that ends with the fresh beginning of another New Year. This year like most in my past, I intend to take this time to complete a comprehensive self-examination. I intend to review my personal goals and tweak them as is prudent. At the same time, I will perform a values check to make sure my compass is operating appropriately.

Our life journey is the most important voyage we take; yet many of us fail to invest in making sure we take control of it. Most of us would not consider getting in our cars without knowing where we were going and the route we intended to take to get to our destination.

In our life journey, goals replace the destinations, and the values are the surrogate for the routes we intend to take to reach those pinnacles. All of this is for you and you alone. As such they can be written on a small piece of paper and kept visible. I normally recommend that we find an important stakeholder to help ensure that our goals are achievable yet aspirational and our values are sound.

These stakeholders might know that a *bridge is out* on the *route* we are contemplating, or our *destination* is a venue that is *unhealthy*. These stakeholders must be capable of delivering great candor as without its use these accountability partners tend to mollify their value.

Good luck on your life journey. Make it exhilarating and self-fulfilling. Only you can define what exhilarating and self-fulfilling means as it applies to your life journey.

REFLECTION 22

A Random Act of Kindness

Recently I learned of a man who was diagnosed with terminal cancer at age 56, who decided to chronicle the last months of his life in a Reflection. Rather than wallow in self-pity this remarkable individual elected to use his situation to inspire as many as he could reach.

According to my source, this individual readily discussed the travails of fighting cancer, while always framing those stories in and around the remarkable life experiences he had the good fortune to realize. He wrote about his family, career, education, and recreational activities. He further addressed the lifetime of support he had received from his church family. As he saw it they were with him every step of the way through good times and bad times alike.

In his final Reflection, knowing death was near, he asked all of his followers to perform an act of random kindness that day. He went on to describe what this might include: buying someone's dinner who is in the line behind at a fast-food restaurant, or traveling to a nursing home and sitting with someone who is alone. As I recall, he had a fairly long list of potential random acts of kindness. I was amazed that he had the courage and strength to draft such a thoughtful missive in his last days.

I was so inspired by the story I thought I would share it with my audience. As I reflected on the entire circumstance, I thought on how we could apply this to our businesses. I realized that I have been blessed to be part of some businesses that had been a part of some impressive community outreach programs.

Interestingly enough, it's very much a symbiotic situation. In order to create an environment where a company or a business can contribute to the betterment of the community that company needs to be successful. At the same time, those intrinsic *random acts of kindness* that companies perform fuel the enthusiasm within the organization that transcends throughout the community creating an environment where the company has more opportunity to win and become successful.

I believe as business leaders we need to pay it forward and take the first step toward community stewardship. Today, in memory of the man whose name I do not know, perform a random act of kindness. You'll win in more ways than you can count.

REFLECTION 23

Blessings Abound You Simply Need to Seek

I received a notice on facebook yesterday that I was tagged in a note. I didn't think much about it. Today, I opened the link and found that a coworker from 14 years ago had mentioned me as someone for whom they were grateful. I immediately was filled with a great sense of happiness. To say this person made my day would be an understatement. Plain and simply I feel blessed.

I commenced to reflect on the many blessings that have been bestowed upon me over my life and fairly quickly became overwhelmed with the number and magnitude. Even those things that seem insurmountable at the time can become blessings when we approach them appropriately.

While at the gym last week I learned of a person who had been in a severe car accident. This too was a blessing. When he was transported to the hospital the attending physician discovered cancer that if left untreated would have been terminal.

Each of us chooses how to react to those events that become part of the fabric of our life journey. We can choose to embrace them and learn. On the contrary, we can wallow in our sorrows and transcend into a site of bitterness.

I enjoy one exercise, in particular, where I have clients write down the ten biggest challenges they face. Next, I ask them to seal it in an envelope and address it to themselves. Then I ask them to have a trusted friend or advisor mail it to them in one year. This exercise is always liberating as normally the vast majority of challenges my clients faced a year previous have been forgotten.

Unfortunately, clients are often plagued by a new list of concerns. The exercise helps clients to realize that seemingly unbeatable challenges are not nearly as devastating as they first thought – but merely part of life's journey.

We all have peaks and valleys in our lives. I believe the valleys come our way so we can better appreciate the peaks.

When each of us adopts a positive attitude and explores opportunities – blessings abound. As we enter into the New Year, take a bit of time to reflect on all the blessings in your life. Happy New Year.

REFLECTION 24

Nelson Mandela: 1918 - 2013

This week the world lost a man who earned the moniker of the most inspirational and courageous person of our times. I learned of his passing while in mid stride on an elliptical trainer in Quapaw, Oklahoma. As I completed my workout, I recalled many of his quotations and how they had guided me through my journey.

His quotes will stimulate all who read them. Whether a business leader, student, homemaker, politician or freedom , we all have a great deal to learn from Nelson Mandela. Some of his quotes follow. Be inspired.

> Resentment is like drinking poison and then hoping
> it will kill your enemies.
>
> Do not judge me by my successes, judge me by
> how many times I fell down and got back up again.
>
> It always seems impossible until it's done.
>
> One of the things I learned when I was negotiating was that
> until I changed myself, I could not change others.

FIRESTARTER

Education is the most powerful weapon that
you can use to change the world.

Appearances matter — and remember to smile.

Courage is not the absence of fear — it's inspiring others
to move beyond it.

After climbing a great hill, one only finds that
there are many more hills to climb.

Know your enemy — and learn about his favorite sport.

It is not where you start, but how high you aim
that matters for success.

When the water starts boiling it is foolish to turn off the heat

We must use time creatively, and forever realize that
the time is always ripe to do right.

A good head and a good heart are always
a formidable combination.

Once a person is determined to help themselves,
there is nothing that can stop them.

A winner is a dreamer who never gives up.

There is no passion to be found in playing small –
in settling for a life less than you are capable of living.

REFLECTION 25

Behavioral Problems - Four Classifications

I am dedicating the next few weeks of Reflections to identify and deal with individuals on the team that can destroy the company's culture and derail the train of success. This could also be referred to as dealing with misfits.

There is a wide spectrum of perpetrators that can be classified as not fitting with the company values and or not performing up to the company expectations. Many of these are extremely easy to identify and resolve. For example, the person who is grouchy and performs poorly is fairly easy to recognize and since most do not particularly like this individual it is an easy task to take the action to exit them from the business. This person would fall into the classification of *does not perform* and *does not fit*.

There are three other broad classifications. The antithesis to *does not perform* and *does not fit* is; *performs and fits*. These individuals are also fairly straightforward to solve. We cherish them, reward them and make sure they know we appreciate them. We need to ensure we do not lose these gems.

The third classification is *fits the company values but does not perform*. Individuals in this classification are a bit more of a challenge to coach. The first element we must understand what is driving the poor performance. There are three general areas to explore.

Is the role wrong for this individual? For example, do we have a person assigned to a role that requires a great level of detail but the person does not excel in that realm.

Is there something going on in this individual's life outside of work that is fueling the poor performance? Some examples include new babies at home, financial trouble, relationship issues and personal and family illness.

Is there something in the work environment or the work itself that is fueling the poor performance? This could include relationship challenges with coworkers, environmental issues in the workspace, a lack of training or a misunderstanding on how to approach the work.

We should explore the drivers and work with the incumbent to see if we can resolve them, or at least identify them and understand how to minimize their impact on performance. In most cases I have found it is very worthwhile to try to coach up those that fit the company values but are struggling with performance. It is much harder to find individuals that are a good values fit than it is to find good performers.

Next we will focus on the fourth and most difficult category of individuals. These are people who perform but do not fit the company values. We tend to want to make excuses for their poor behavior because we love the results they deliver. Regularly it is extremely difficult to identify these carcinomas – and to deal with them can be a bigger challenge.

As you will learn in the upcoming weeks, I strongly believe that you exit these misfits from your organization and ensure everyone knows why. When in doubt, throw them out.

Stay Tuned...

REFLECTION 26

Behavioral Problems – Session #1: Candor Charlatans

If you have been following my *Reflections*, or have had the opportunity to read my book, you will know that I believe one of the biggest challenges facing businesses today is lack of candor. In order to transform your organization to a candor juggernaut you must first develop a high level of trust throughout the team. Without trust, instilling candor will not work effectively.

When you introduce the concept of candor as a core competency be vigilant for the rise of candor charlatans. Candor charlatans come in many sizes and shapes, but they all have one thing in common: they claim to eagerly embrace the concept of candor and usually are the first ones to commence the misuse of candor while making sure anyone within earshot knows that they are champions of candor.

Just as a poor poker player will *tell* their opponent the value of his or her hand, candor charlatans usually signal their charade. The most common signal is that they feel compelled to state that *this is candor* or *this is how candor works*.

Regularly, these imposters use the candor mantra to vocalize complaints or to punish coworkers who they feel have *wronged* them. A quick test is to evaluate statements of claimed candor and determine if these statements vindicate their actions at the expense of others, or if the subject matter is intended to benefit the pretender.

Another way to recognize a candor charlatan is if they are unable to accept receiving critical candor concerning their own behavior or actions. At their worst, the candor charlatan besmirches the staff, particularly -those who are not in his or her reporting sphere, creating significant chasms of mistrust. While on their mission to destroy any hope of organizational cooperation, the mere suggestion that they rethink some of their actions sends them into a tailspin of denial, only serving to *amp up* the disruptive behavior.

The challenge with candor charlatans is frequently they are executives who have delivered good results. As Jim Collins appropriately advises, *good is the enemy of great*. As such, candor charlatans need to be expunged from the organization, and the most courageous of leaders will make sure that the team knows why.

REFLECTION 27

Behavioral Problems – Session #2: The Entitled Elitist

Most agree that entitlement is a dirty word in business. In fact, executives are challenged to ensure entitlement does not creep into the organization on a regular basis. Unfortunately, leaders frequently only search for signs of entitlement at the lowest levels of the organization.

In doing so, stop watches are employed to make sure plant operators do not exceed their 15 minute break while executives convince themselves that a two hour lunch with three martinis on the company tab is perfectly acceptable.

I am not an advocate for loosened work practices, but I am an enthusiast for ensuring companies adopt even handed approaches when dealing with all levels within the organization. Far too often leaders turn a blind eye to the behavioral issues exhibited by individuals within their own sphere. It takes intense discipline to avoid entitlement, and when it comes to a select group of executives the self-discipline just doesn't exist – and in the worst cases perpetrators become inflamed when questioned.

Let's examine a couple of parallel examples. Employee A is a long-time worker in production and he sleeps in and is five minutes late for his shift. Normally, established work rules predispose his or her fate – the dreaded point in the attendance system. If he or she repeats this behavior it could lead to termination and in many cases justifiably so.

Employee E is an executive and arrives ten minutes late for a 1 p.m. team meeting. He has an excuse: his workout ran a bit over at the gym. Regularly, a joke is made about how buff his arms are and the meeting proceeds without incident. The true problem is he is regularly late and it's often more than 10 minutes.

Normally no questions are asked, but in the rare event they are there is a ready excuse. "I had to get my workout in and I have a plane to catch tonight." This can be followed by, "Need I remind you of the company wellness initiative?"

The problem is that when you have an entitled elitist within your ranks it does not stop with a single event or a couple of events. These individuals start to believe that the rules do not apply to them and further tend to suppose that certain entitlements are due them. This leads to outrageous expenditures on travel, excesses in administrative support, and a Bacchanalia of creature comforts all funded by the company.

You may convince yourself that this individual is so important to the mission of the enterprise that the company simply cannot afford to lose him or her. We convince ourselves, *If we do not afford these excesses they will run to the competition.* I believe the departure of these folks should be celebrated, and frankly it should be at the company's bequest and as promptly as possible.

Still don't get the risk? Let's dive a bit deeper. Administrative personnel have to arrange for the travel and process the expense reports. Employees at all levels are observant and experience improper behavior (many times very similar behavior for which they have been punished in the past), and others in support roles have their workload increased due to the required hand holding. This erodes morale faster than any activity I can think of and is the fuel for union organizing as the struggle between the *haves* and *have nots* is readily apparent.

Fellow executives have challenged me that others should simply get over it, and add that it is no one's business. I would challenge that while none of us is wired exactly the same, most find it extremely difficult to turn a blind eye, particularly when a 2% annual pay increase had to be delayed due to the company missing their annual number. Further, I would argue that waste and excess is everyone's business.

I will close this Reflection with a funny yet tragic experience from my past. A company received a four figure invoice from an overnight shipping company for an employee's golf clubs that they had been hired to air freight. When challenged, the employee claimed he was concerned that the airline would lose the clubs and he might not have them in time for the customer outing he was attending. Upon further investigation it was revealed that the flight was a nonstop and the threat of loss didn't explain the air freight return of the clubs to his home or the courier fee to have the resort handle the clubs upon their arrival and prepare them for their return journey.

Need this guy in your organization? I think not – and it's more common that you will want to admit.

REFLECTION 28

Behavioral Problems – Session #3:
Drawing a Crowd

But at What Cost?

Most of us have heard the comment: "He (She) really knows how to draw a crowd." Or "He (she) drew a crowd." No doubt these people have a real gift. They are likable, funny, and charismatic and can command an audience. On the surface they seem almost perfect, and regularly these folks are great assets and can become valued team members. On the flip side, the talents that these *entertainers* have been blessed with can come with a dangerous curse.

Oftentimes these individuals become so invested in their delightful, robust, enthusiastic, and whimsical personalities that they are not able to turn their *show* off. They are so energized by their euphoria spawned by the roaring crowd that they are driven to experience more. This regularly results in inappropriate behavior that tears the team apart while ruining any chance for organizational cooperation.

At its worst these individuals are like a two-sided coin – dazzling yet disruptive; resourceful yet reckless; energetic yet entitled; witty yet woeful. Like a moth to a flame you are drawn in only to get burnt. Their charisma masks the damage created from their sophomoric behavior. *Oh that just comes with the territory*, we convince ourselves.

Excuses lead to organizational discord as others on the team laugh along, while they wonder what is said about them when they are not in the room. Unchecked, these shenanigans erode trust and impair performance.

Chances are there is one or two of these types in your organization. Their superficial charm and likable personalities have leaders question how to deal with these characters. As is often the case these folks are regularly in middle or senior management and are astute enough to make sure their shenanigans don't impugn other senior managers. Actually it's quite simple: expunge them from your organization and tell the entire team why. If you want some laughs buy the team tickets to the local comedy club.

REFLECTION 29

Behavioral Problems – Session #4: The Resolute Manager (The Office Bully)

For the past several weeks we have been exploring many challenges faced by companies who fail to recognize that team performance is hampered by individuals who have serious behavioral deficiencies. They allow these individuals to remain within their employ and in roles where they create chaos and crush enthusiasm.

These are the people on the team that appear to deliver but do not fit our values. They are cancers who if left untreated kill any chance for a thriving team.

I saved the resolute manager for last as they can be among the worst. These individuals regularly reign with iron fists and use threats and fear as their chosen motivators. The word reign is highly appropriate in this case because regularly these people come to believe that they are sovereign.

Regularly, the teams controlled by these types of autocrats deliver seemingly positive results. As such, incumbents are regularly lauded for their performance. I've even seen executives hold up these types for their exemplary performance. In doing so the cycle continues to the detriment of the entire enterprise.

Here is the folly, it is true that fear is a great motivator; however, it is in fact the number one root cause for behavioral challenges. Unfortunately, motivation through fear is extremely transactional. There can be no true loyalty fostered when threats and bullying are the norm.

I've seen baseball bats handed out as motivators. At one point in my career I even was amused by the notion. How wrong I was. The damage this type of foolishness does to the team dynamics is numbing.

When we opt for leaders who motivate with recognition and rewards we create a positive environment where the art of the possible is celebrated. In these environments trust is nurtured, and intense loyalty is the product.

Certainly, there is a time and place for negative reinforcement but when we staff our team with players who share our values those times and places are very few and far between. Negative reinforcement transition into coachable moments. Instead of beating down we can coach up and in the process educate and stimulate enhanced performance.

REFLECTION 30

The Orchestra Conductor

Over the next several weeks, I am going to focus on leadership. In my book I refer to leaders as orchestra conductors. I think that the metaphor remains sound, but there is so much more involved to becoming a great leader that I am searching for a more comprehensive moniker. Alas, I have yet to come up with one I like better. As such, we are going to stay with the orchestra conductor as our chosen metaphor.

The leader is the conductor of the orchestra. The conductor's job is to bring all the instruments together to create beautiful music. You can't lead the orchestra if you are trying to play the piccolo. Go and find the best player of each instrument, and teach them to create beautiful sounds together. Conductors conduct; musicians perform.

The greatest musician may also be a great conductor, but more times than not, it is better if they work to hone their craft on their chosen instrument and leave the conducting to the conductor. Knowing if a great musician has the ability to conduct is the key to a successful migration to conductor.

The mistake many businesses make is they value results and as a consequence, individuals who have delivered in the past are often selected as the leaders of tomorrow. In many cases it works out well, but quite often these top performers do not possess the proper attributes to become a great leader.

"We can teach them to be leaders," is a common phrase. I am a huge fan of education but I really do not believe you can teach leadership. You are either predisposed to be a good leader or you're not. You can teach leadership skills to help with the development of an individual who has the innate ability to become a great leader, but you can't create a leader where one does not exist.

In my view, the greatest leaders are the ones who realize that they are not the greatest, but they have the ability to develop the greatest performance from their team. Moreover, they realize that their leadership status is a blessing, not a right.

Hang with me for the next few weeks and we will explore leadership in more depth. I think you will find the exercise worth your time.

REFLECTION 31

Humility: The Single Most Important Leadership Attribute

I've often wondered what it would be like to be a superstar professional athlete. Fifty thousand fans are screaming your name with millions of adoring fans watching on television. When you bring home a victory you become almost "deified." Better yet a champion. It must be an intense feeling. I see it as very dangerous territory.

Having not ever experienced that status I have become extremely sympathetic with their plight. When a superstar gets into trouble I regularly ask if I would have had the humility to have resisted the spoils of fame had it been bestowed upon me. Simply stated I hope so but I don't know so. *Walk a mile in my shoes* is normally associated with tough times, but I believe it applies to all times and particularly times of great success.

The fact is that in most cases leaders make significant investments to gain their status as leader. Who could blame them if they wanted to bask in the fruits of their labor? To make the transition to a great leader one must relegate their basking to private moments and opt to celebrate those that have contributed to their success. Let's not forget to thank God, our family, our mentors, and the teammates who have toiled for us as we climbed the so-called ladder of success.

All of us were brought into this world in the same fashion, with a single breath of air and we will leave with a final one. Along the way we get to experience a multitude of different encounters and opportunities. How we conduct ourselves is what defines us. How did we treat our fellow man?

Many of us are more blessed or luckier than others and things seem to fall into place. Others have the drive to overcome the obstacles in their lives. Others are satisfied just participating in the experience. We all are a bit different, but we all come from the same humble beginnings.

Far too often, in the world of private assistants, special travel perks, and a seat in the rarified air of the board room the leader begins to believe that he or she is *special*. Once one opts to travel along this path their identity goes through a dangerous metamorphosis. More importantly, if leaders do not possess a good dose of humility, their teams see right through them. The team may execute each transaction flawlessly, but without the connection between leader and team the journey will always be rocky. This is not a popularity contest, but rather an understanding between leader and team that as people they are equals no matter what their title might be.

It is important that we do not confuse the concept of equality as individuals with the superior position the leader holds within the organization. The leader is the final decision maker and while understanding the power of humility, he or she can never allow themselves to become friends with members of the team. Being reachable by the team is encouraged, but the leader must keep a productive level of distinction between their position and the rest of the team all while treating every member of the team with dignity and respect.

Treating your fellow teammates with dignity and respect has nothing to do with going out to the bar and drinking with them. Ensuring that you make the next pot of coffee when it's your turn should not be confused with passing internet jokes around the office. Seeking an employee out to ask how their sick parent is doing or how their son or daughter's sports team did over the weekend is a far cry from gossiping about the new woman in accounting or the old guy in sales. If we have our humility box checked, we can proceed to review those intangible attributes that make leaders great.

REFLECTION 32

The Decision Maker

Last week we focused on humility and this week we are going to review decision making. Specifically we are talking about tough decisions. Easy decisions are just that – easy. Many individuals that I have worked with have suggested, wrongfully by the way, that decision making and humility are in conflict, adding that making difficult or unpopular decisions are borne of a lack of humility.

I've struggled to make the connection and have come to believe that there is confusion between humility and courage. Making a tough call is much more about having courage than a lack of humility. The motives behind the tough call may very well be a window into a leader's humility.

Remember, leadership is not a popularity contest. It is incredibly difficult for just about everyone to make tough calls, particularly when they directly affect their people. Unless you don't have a heart, you are probably going to agonize about those decisions. If you don't have a heart, you have no business being a leader.

So, it's a given that making these tough calls will turn your stomach inside out and likely result in many sleepless nights. You are not unique; there is no crime in being afraid or sympathetic. The crime is committed when you allow this fear or sympathy to slow your decision making process or change your decision to the detriment of the company. You must act swiftly and deftly.

Get the tough call behind you and move on with life. While it is certainly permissible to talk compassionately about the difficulty of the decision, shirking the responsibility to others is unacceptable. You need to take the responsibility and clearly and concisely explain the rationale for the decision. If you cannot clearly or concisely explain it, you are not ready to make the decision.

The more negatively you believe the decision will be received by your team, the more important it is that you have your key leaders on board with you. Even if they personally disagree with the decision being made, you must insist that they endorse it publicly. Nothing creates more angst in an organization than when key leaders question a decision with other team members.

It's okay for them to say, "I don't expect you to like this decision, but it is the best thing we can do under the circumstances." I have found that it is the second and third layer of management that normally causes more difficulty than the lower level employees in the organization. People are much more resilient than many leaders expect and provided the communication is forthright and the rationale is explained, team members normally understand. There is no correlation between liking and accepting a decision.

It is of vital importance that you and your closest team members must conduct themselves with total impartiality with all employees. You cannot be perceived as being inequitable. In fact, you need to demand your top executives lead by example. Nothing kills morale more than when executives are communicating a tough decision and are seen as excluding themselves from the implications of that decision. This plays itself out regularly when executives announce a drastic cost-cutting program, maybe including wage freezes but are then spotted at the finest restaurant in town later that evening.

Also vital to announcing a challenging decision is total transparency. Tell everyone on the team why a decision is being made, make sure they understand that you have carefully considered many options and how the decision will positively impact the future. Do not fall into the trap of attempting to spin the story to make the situation sound nicer than it is. Almost everyone sees through these facades and it erodes your credibility moving forward.

John Wooden said; "Tell the truth. That way you don't have to remember a story." Great advice from one of the greatest leaders of our time.

REFLECTION 33

You Claim to Listen but Did You Hear

Great leaders need to be awesome listeners. Most leaders claim to be great at listening, but do they really hear? Hearing means you transform your listening into action that demonstrates that you have heard. This is particularly important when you are attempting to connect with every level of your organization. I describe this as being a good ear.

To be a good ear you must understand that leaders need to be in touch with all their people. You must understand that what excites you may not excite your employees. Frankly, as spring arrives you might be trying to decide what golf course you are going to play this weekend and they may be attempting to determine how they are going to pay last month's gas bill due to the harsh winter. Every leader will be exposed to some uncomfortable topics, specifically the ones most people do not like to talk about. How they address these topics will suggest the quality of leader they are.

One of the challenges is that regularly leaders have not had the opportunity to live through the economic strife that most endure at some point in their life, or they have simply forgotten what it was like to be in that position. Regardless of your socioeconomic past, we are all able to learn how to connect with our employees, but it takes a discipline few are willing to follow. It means actually working at the job that your lowest level person completes every day of his or her life.

This does not mean spending a day in the field and afterward you go out for a nice lobster dinner. This means getting your hands dirty on a regular basis doing the actual work that you are asking others to do. Understanding what their day-to-day is like and truly empathizing with their struggles. It's incredibly enlightening and rewarding if you are willing to do it. Of course, you will have your regular work to do during this period of time so these exercises might come in spurts of two and three hour increments. Two or three hours on the packaging line or in the receiving pit will give you a perspective like no other.

Once connected with your team you will realize many things that may have escaped you. You will learn that the vast majority of employees in your organization work only to maintain a standard of living that allows them to strive for a better life for their children. They are deeply committed and loyal, but they rely on you as the leader to make the right decisions. The paradox is that they have no idea what it is you actually do.

When you connect with your people they will come to you with their problems. This can be dangerous territory, but if managed properly, this communication is very powerful and can be a huge advantage against unproductive behavior.

One of Colin Powell's leadership principles is, "The day soldiers stop bringing you their problems is the day you have stopped leading them. They have either lost confidence that you can help them or concluded that you do not care. Either case is a failure of leadership."

We can apply this same sentiment to business. If your employees stop sharing their thoughts and concerns with you, you are failing to lead. Allowing your people to think you're incompetent or uncaring is not acceptable.

The other side of being a good listener is understanding that, due to the success you've had as a leader, you have huge influence that spreads across the organization. You may not feel any differently but many people will be intimidated by you and your position. Consequently, you must make an extra effort to connect.

Great leaders learn how to listen and hear. They demonstrate that they have done both by their actions. You should pattern your leadership style to make this happen. Simply find a way to incorporate this skill set into your style. If you think you are already great at it, ask yourself when was the last time someone with whom you do not regularly communicate came to your office and told you something you really did not want to hear. If it hasn't happened with some regularity then you have not learned to connect.

REFLECTION 34

Leaders Coach Up and Coach Out

Leaders are great coaches. They use candor and discipline, along with a confidence-building reassurance to develop their teams. All people are created equal, but all employees are not.

Even the best teams will have some members that are more talented and others that are struggling. The leader must be viewed as unbiased and equitable in dealing with each member of the team.

Leaders need to have the courage to exit those from the team who are not great team players, even if they are potential superstars. I refer to this as coaching out. As we have covered in previous Reflections. Allowing team members who do not fit to *hang around* is equivalent to living with cancer and taking no action. Eventually it will kill the team.

Leaders should also have the insight and acumen to push the team members to the next level; pushing the best and the brightest as hard, if not harder, than the weakest. This is known as coaching up. Even the best budding superstars need to be molded. Proper coaching will transform a good prospect into a great leader.

Great leaders know that the best teams are an amalgamation of individuals, each with their own unique skills, experiences and capabilities, brought together for a common purpose and goal. Coaches realize the results of the entire team far outweigh the individual performances of their team members.

They are careful to recognize individual performances, but they are quick to view these achievements publicly through a team lens. Save individual praise for one-on-one sessions. Great leaders develop and encourage maturity in their best performers, so they embrace the quiet victories of their individual performances. Individuals on your team who have the character to understand and thrive on this approach are candidates to become the future leaders of your organization.

Too often, recognition is given only to superstar individuals after astounding performances. Great coaches realize it is important to cultivate an environment where all employees are acknowledged for giving their best. This will increase morale and prompt team members to do their best work every day, not just when large, prestigious initiatives are being undertaken. Even failures should be celebrated if indeed the person gave their very best. If you are in the business of inflating already bloated egos of a few elite performers, you're not coaching at the highest level.

In my view, the greatest leaders understand that they too need coaching. "It's lonely at the top." is a common phrase. A good coach will keep the leader grounded and most importantly alert him or her when he or she is *wearing no clothes*.

REFLECTION 35

The Great Simplifier

Many businesses struggle to realize the pinnacle of success because their leaders tend to overcomplicate almost every task. Normally it is a lack of self-confidence, fear or lack of trust in coworkers that drive this unproductive behavior. Unproductive complexity is introduced into most decision making. This introduces drag that stymies organizational capacity and inhibits organizational cooperation.

Great leaders have the uncanny ability to be great simplifiers. The more seemingly complicated a challenge, the harder the leader works to reduce it to the most common terms. This is a key to the "Unbundle It®" way of life.

Simplification starts with elimination of variables. The easiest way to describe this concept is to look at algebraic equations. Most would agree that a math problem with one variable is fairly easy to solve. When we introduce two variables, we need significantly more information, but as with the one variable equation, it is a fairly easy solve.

When we get to three variable equations, we start to add a level of complexity that requires significantly more information and effort to solve. While it may not be accurate to describe the complexity in moving from two variables to three as logarithmic, it is certainly much more precise than using the direct three-divided-by-two approach, which falsely assumes that it is merely fifty percent harder to solve.

In business the biggest challenges normally have dozens of variables all moving in their own direction independent of the others. In many cases, the problems are so complicated that a cry to find the root cause is sounded. Unfortunately, there can be many root causes and along the way red herrings will move the team in the wrong direction.

Great leaders direct their team to attempt to hold as many variables constant as possible and then to examine the situation through a single variable. In doing so, the team can quickly discount those pseudo root causes and focus on the key driver or drivers of the problem.

Leaders must be careful to avoid falling into the trap of getting too immersed in the corrective action process. They need to be a source that remains above the fray and watches vigilantly as the team searches for a solution. The old adage "we can't see the forest through the trees" is an apt statement when it comes to the leader's role. He or she must remain out of the trees.

Great leaders find the simplicity in every complexity. Poor leaders will introduce complexity into every simplicity.

REFLECTION 36

Great Leaders Teach and Yearn to be Taught

Far too often leaders become complacent or self-absorbed and forget that education is one of the most important keys to success. They come to believe that they have *seen it all* and as such *have all the answers*. Further, they fail to recognize the importance of both formal and informal education.

Great leaders are huge fans of education. Leaders use failures and victories alike as teachable moments. They find ways to creatively ensure their team and its individual members learn from history. They apply the learning into living and breathing educational tools that can be used long into the future.

Leaders are always looking for creative ways to educate. They are particularly adept at teaching others how to adapt learning from a key experience to other opportunities or hurdles to be leapt. Something that worked in one situation may be the perfect solution in another.

Further, they are zealots for formal team member education. They are on the lookout for assignment appropriate formal education programs and ensure that each year ample funding is allocated for same.

As with great teachers, great leaders must not only be willing to be educated but, in fact, seek out opportunities to enhance their breadth of edification. They are inquisitive, constantly challenging the experts and digging into the details to find new solutions. I believe a day that a leader does not learn something is a day lost.

Great leaders are always looking for opportunities to learn. They are adept at applying learning to multiple scenarios. If a leader is not actively seeking to find opportunities to learn, they are probably missing out on many educational experiences.

Every leader should insist on a robust formal educational program as part of their annual plan. This, coupled with a leader driven culture of continuous ad hoc education embedded into the skin of the organization will deliver astounding results. Great leaders learn quickly that education is a winner.

REFLECTION 37

The Risk Taker

Career politicians seem to me to be excellent examples of the epitome of poor leaders. They tend to wait until they see the results of the latest poll prior to taking a stand. Further, they change their positions based mostly on their self-preservation. Simply stated their continuing careers outweigh the greater good.

Similar to a politician, a leader who must have everything proven to them before making a decision creates a very boring environment that tends to demotivate the team. Certainly, taking wild risks is not advisable and would be considered irresponsible, but going with your gut and challenging conventional wisdom creates an exciting environment where opportunities abound.

Leaders from companies where risk taking is not encouraged may deliver seemingly positive results, but at the same time, they leave material amounts of revenue and profit untapped. They operate in a malaise, waiting for others to create the disruption in the marketplace.

It is no easy task to determine which opportunities to chase, but great leaders tend to use a couple of rules to guide their decision making. The first rule is if the opportunity is at least fifty percent or more attractive from a return on the investment than the average of the portfolio or the expectation of the shareholders then it should be considered as a very attractive prospect.

For example if you lead a company and your portfolio averages twenty percent annual return on investment and a project, whether it be a new product launch or a capital investment, creates a thirty percent or better return after all factors have been considered, it definitely is worthy of a complete evaluation. Another way to look at it is if there is a three year anticipated payback on a project it should receive significant attention.

Companies that take measured risk and create disruption in the marketplace are rewarded with higher than average valuations, but they must learn to become proficient risk takers. If we use our model of fifty percent better returns than the average portfolio, we allow ourselves room for some mistakes.

The second filter in determining your confidence level is that the decision or investment is the correct one. If you are more than sixty-seven percent confident of success, this investment would trigger strong consideration for a decision to go forward. Let's assume that your gut is right, two thirds of the time applying the fifty percent premium factor delivers exactly your historical performance. In effect, the downside risk is very low if you apply these two filters. In a sense you have hedged your bet.

The time and expense you have saved your company is material and affords you the opportunity to investigate other prospects. Simply stated, you have just created a much more effective organization that has greatly expanded capacity.

There are two very important concerns to watch for when taking risks. The first is that your key stakeholders must be passionate about the risks to be taken. Lack of passion will likely relegate the opportunity to a failed status.

The second is to ensure you do not become so invested in the opportunity that you waste resources and money trying to chase a bad opportunity. You are going to have failures if you follow this risk-based approach. Have preset targets and benchmarks prior to commencing and watch them closely. If you do not meet important deliverables, have the maturity to either change on the fly or kill the project.

Great leaders take risks, challenge the status quo, and go with their gut. Hiring a bunch of experts to tell you how to proceed is like giving them your watch and having them tell you what time it is. There is a time and a place for consultants. Evaluate your core competencies and consider engaging outside experts when you are out of your area of expertise. When an issue you are struggling with is not a core competency, that is the time when hiring an outside advisor may be the proper decision.

Leaders who reward risk taking create exciting environments where team members are engaged and motivated and great wealth is created. Working for a company led by these types of leaders is like being part of an action movie – exhilarating and electrifying.

BONUS REFLECTION #1

Breakfast with Jack Welch

Ten years ago, I attended a Jack Welch event. In true Jack spirit he had arranged for a luck of draw seating at dinner. A bowl with scraps of paper was used. Those receiving a 1 would be seated at Jack's table. Those with a 2 would sit at his wife's table. I decided that if fortune was in the offing it would be in the hands of others. As such I waited until a lone scrap of paper remained – on it a 1.

The table held ten people and nine seats were occupied when I arrived. In a second stroke of luck the seat on Jack's immediate right remained vacant. This was truly fortuitous as I would never have been so bold to select a seat adjacent to Jack if other options had presented themselves.

The next morning I sat alone at breakfast studying some course materials. I was shocked when Jack asked if he could join me. We had an hour together where he probed me with tough questions that I found exhilarating and awe inspiring. He asked about my business, passions, and failures. He asked me specifically what kept me up at night. I thought for a second or two and shared with him that my biggest concern was a totally unforeseen disaster. I added that with my team and some inkling that an event was possible or probable we could leap any hurdle. Jack smiled in approval.

Since that hour I have been inspired to push through any fears that I have had about my background or capabilities. In Jack, I found a person who was just like me and likely just like you. A straight-shooting Irishman who in his words *wants a burger and a beer* for lunch. Comfortable in his own skin, he had an ability to make others equally happy in theirs.

Later that morning Jack announced to the one hundred and twenty in attendance that he had enjoyed breakfast with me and urged others to seek me out. Not the kind of press I was looking for, but I became quite popular in the break periods.

He signed my copy of Winning and in it he wrote three words. "Keep Feeding Them." Was it a reference to my pet category career, or was it deeper? I believe it was an invitation for me to keep *feeding* my passions.

Jack Welch, a regular guy who accomplished extraordinary things. With his passing I share his words to me with my colleagues – find your "Them" and "Keep Feeding"

BONUS REFLECTION #2

In Memory Kobe Bryant

Watching the coverage on the tragic passing of Kobe Bryant I heard an interview where Kobe stated the following.

"I want people to think of me as a talented overachiever. I was blessed with talent. But I worked as if I had none."

I found this quotation as one of the more inspirational and universally applicable as I've encountered. In life it is essential that we all determine where our talent lies and vigorously apply it to meet our life purpose. Recognition of our talents, the courage to use them, and the discipline to prepare as if we have none is sage advice. In basketball or business this sentiment rings true. Business Olympians might not find fame, but the fulfillment is omnipresent.

Further reflection brought these words of John Wooden to my mind. "Talent is God given. Be humble. Fame is man-given. Be grateful. Conceit is self-given. Be careful."

I've imagined a heaven-based conversation between Kobe and John. No question, basketball just got a whole lot more interesting in heaven today.

EPILOGUE

So Many Fires to Kindle

By the time the editors are finished with this work, I will be in my 43rd year of leading in one fashion or another. In many ways, I cannot even think of a time that the leadership principles that I've learned and incorporated into my style have not influenced my actions. Along the way, I became infatuated with the concept of being a firestarter. In many ways, the compulsion to ignite has become my driving force.

In a true paradox, that young hesitant man I once was – who purposely planned his life without any consideration or desire to become a leader – has become addicted to leadership, along with the well-being it has created within my soul. Simply stated, I am drawn to lead.

Today, my desire to ignite has manifested in a whirlwind of activity. I continue to serve on boards in and around the animal nutrition industry. The road has been a winding one, but I know that it's the market segment I was destined to join.

I'm drawn to coaching, and I am always looking to help mold new souls. It's incredibly fulfilling. I look forward to helping people leap the hurdles in front of them, while offering constant encouragement. I tell them that their life journey is a marathon, not a sprint. And I remind them that most of the seemingly insurmountable challenges that they face today are merely insignificant speed bumps on their road to abundance.

I find myself involved in youth mentoring organizations. The excitement I experience when I work with youth is hard to describe. I can assure you that the bounty of blessings I have enjoyed has far exceeded my investment.

Your journey as a leader will most assuredly have its share of bumps, curves, and noteworthy routes. Remember that the journey should be about becoming the best version of the person you were destined to be. When you find yourself comfortable in your own skin, you will recognize that you have arrived at the stopping point in your journey – at exactly the right time and the right place.

This is not the end; but rather, a new beginning. Fuel up and get ready to explore the next chapter of this most amazing journey known as life. As you depart, please consider the following:

Be courageous in all things. Having the courage to stand with your convictions can be a challenge, but it will pay significant rewards as you migrate through your journey. When you choose the path less traveled, sometimes it will be excruciating, but it may still be the right path to create the achievements and legacy of your lifetime.

Continue to foster your insatiable curiosity. Always ask questions. Engage others through your genuine interest in their story and in the events that have marked their sojourn on this Earth.

Commit to learning something new every day. In doing so, promise to share your knowledge with all who have interest. Education is a two-way street. We need to possess the drive to become educated with the same vigor that we seek to educate others.

Epilogue

The combination of humility and empathy is very rare – nourish it. Empathy and humility do not equal weakness. Boldness and audaciousness are not contrary to either principle.

Take calculated risks. Trust your gut and your team members. It will simply make the journey more exciting. And excitement will attract the best and brightest to join you in your quest.

Keep in mind that a coach can literally be a game-changer. A kick in the backside and a pat on the back will have equal impact on those around you. Use both with great regularity, but only when required. The pats can be public, but the kicks should be delivered privately.

Remember that intense discipline will make you better. Discipline will help the team advance, and will unlock a mountain of time that previously was unavailable. When discipline is deployed impartially, the team excels. Building trust among team members is a foundational priority, and trust is fostered when discipline and impartiality is on full display.

Never forget that great leaders are great communicators. Communication is omnipresent, but words matter. Choose them wisely. Seek to engage your people on a regular basis, and be prepared to listen and demonstrate that you have heard them.

Communicate your vision regularly. Your message should be a simple and optimistic one. We are setting course to the place where we are destined to go – and when we arrive, it will be awesome. Our arrival at any one place is not the end, but a new beginning for us to travel to the next great destination together.

Always be open to advice from others, but never allow that advice to mandate a direction that is contrary to your set of values. It is incredibly tempting to follow the path of least resistance. Often, that easy trail will require you to push aside those things that are important to you. You may find victory, but it may be a hollow one.

In that superficial triumph, you might tarnish something that is much more important – your integrity.

Becoming a leader is a great responsibility. Never try to be someone you are not. Do not emulate a single mentor. Build that unique character that is an amalgamation of your experiences and influences. You are a singular soul, a perfectly imperfect version of the person you were meant to be. Celebrate and enjoy.

Above all else, be a good steward of the blessings you have encountered. Share your wisdom unconditionally. In all things, try to help others to optimize their life journeys. When we seek to make the world a bit better, we change lives. It matters little if we change one life, or millions. What is vital is that we improve the exact number of lives we were meant to influence.

Finally – remember to have fun and never take yourself too seriously. The ego is an interesting phenomenon. The same drive that helps to create a great leader can propel them into the abyss. I recall that vital advice: "It's just dog food. It will be in the lawn in a couple of days."

I am reminded of the incredible blessing of meeting Jack Welch of GE. It was my good fortune that I was able to have him join me for a one-on-one breakfast. In less than an hour, that incredible business leader fired questions my way so quickly that I was awestruck. Each question hit its target and he came to know more about my business and me than most anyone I ever met.

Afterward, he endorsed my copy of his book, Winning. It read, "Keep feeding them. - Jack."

"How wonderful," I mused. "He tied my field of work into this personalized message." I was utterly overcome with joy. The man known as the greatest CEO of the 20th century had found it worthy of his consideration to leave me with a personal message.

Epilogue

A few years later, his message struck a new and different meaning. He had not been referring to dogs and cats. He was reminding me to fuel my passions – and in doing so, to feed the fire. His message took on a whole new and much deeper meaning.

I will close by sharing Jack's inspiration to me with you, the reader. There is a fire within each of you. Foster it, share it, and watch what transpires.

"Keep Feeding Them"

ACKNOWLEDGMENTS

I Am Grateful

I am grateful that God continues to guide me and nurture me, even though I screw up all of the time.

I am grateful for the men and women who defend our country. They make it possible for me to accomplish the things that I have in my life.

I am grateful for my family and the support they provide. My grandchildren are a blessing. Watching them start their journeys is immensely rewarding.

I am grateful for all of the people in my dedication at the beginning of this book. I deeply appreciate their wisdom and support.

I am grateful for my neighbors and friends. You are the best, and my life has been enriched through your love.

I am grateful for the team at O'Leary Publishing. They transform my writing into magic.

www.ingramcontent.com/pod-product-compliance
Lightning Source LLC
Chambersburg PA
CBHW042048280426

4367JCB00087B/480/J